CONTENT STRATEGY FOR BLOGGERS

Learn How To Understand Your Audience And To Create
High-Quality Content That Sells

JACOB GREEN

Jacob Green
The Blog Expert

COPYRIGHT

Table of Contents

Before getting started, as I've said before, there is an expanding pressure on content makers and brands to think of techniques that connect with clients to an ever-increasing extent. Be that as it may, is this the main impetus for them? How about we examine the fundamental advantages of a very much made content procedure:

A decent content system targets making an association between the brand and shoppers. This connection is made when the content contacts the passionate side of the individual devouring it. As we as a whole know, feelings assume a significant job in the purchaser's choice procedure. In light of the effect a brand has at an enthusiastic level, it can change clients into steadfast ones or lose clients until the end of time. Besides, a content procedure customized to the client's advantages, engages the brand, making it hang out before the challenge as progressively pertinent.

At the point when a brand has a rational content procedure, the power it has over its clients is incredibly upgraded. Clearly, it can't direct what the purchaser will or won't do, however, it can shape it in a specific way. Other than this, it can decide purchasers take an all the more dominant position against the issues that influence the general public they live in.

A very much executed content procedure can demonstrate important to your entire correspondence endeavors, as it speaks to the core of your showcasing methodology. Without it, the promoting activities would need content coherency, making it less important to customers. This thus additionally harms the brand.

Normally, an incredible content methodology upgrades the

intensity of the brand and shapes in a specific way purchaser's conduct. Instead of limited time crusades, this procedure doesn't happen in a split second or in an extremely brief period, yet over a more drawn out length of time, the result coming about naturally, and not affected by motivators, for example, a low cost.

All together for the content to be helpful for readers, the procedure must be custom fitted to the client's advantages, while not ignoring the brand's goals. Fundamentally, the procedure must adjust and interface the focused on the crowd's inclinations with the brand's objectives. Along these lines, the content is devoured naturally, without being compellingly pushed by the organization.

Despite the fact that the content is obviously expended naturally, in the present content-rich condition, the correspondence endeavors must be named by an SEO procedure, with the end goal for them to be as compelling as could reasonably be expected.

New content floods the web each second, and with individuals' ability to focus shorter now than at any other time, it is critical for you to share your content precisely where your objective is. This implies you don't need to utilize each online networking stage or each content appropriation stage accessible, however simply the ones that issue. For example, perhaps the best channel for us to speak with our crowd is through our blog. This channel empowers us to give our crowd valuable snippets of data about advanced promoting and web-based life advertising, for example, contextual analyses, forecasts and substantially more.

While actualizing a content procedure, you should choose

which metric is best for you. Along these lines, you can survey how proficient and viable your content is. These markers may vary dependent on your objectives, and will likewise be utilized to modify the system progressively. For example, in the event that you need to build your mindfulness, you can pay special mind to the number of perspectives or adherents. Then again, in the event that you need to upgrade your association with your crowd, you can pay special mind to the number of remarks, shares, the time spent on the page and so forth.

A very much caused content technique can convey fantastic outcomes to both enormous and little organizations. On the off chance that you haven't got one yet, you unquestionably should investigate it and make one. Similarly, as with everything in the online condition, time is a vital factor, so the quicker you start, the better.

A focus on copywriting for bloggers

The vast majority consider copywriting a tool of publicizing where the marketing specialist participates in the compelling artwork of writing to sell a specific item or service. In any case, it is, in reality, more than that. As per Copywriting.com, copywriting is "the workmanship and study of composing words to advance an item, a business, an individual or a thought; and cautiously choosing, altering, weaving and building those words such that they'll convince the reader into making a particular and quantifiable move.

Wait – I recognize what you are going to state.

You are a blogger, not a marketing specialist – for what reason do you have to gain proficiency with so much stuff?

Try not to go off fighting your little heart out at this time. I comprehend what you are stating.

Also, in the relatively recent past, I felt the very same way.

Until I began to see this truly interesting marvel: all the influencers and up and coming bloggers are not just great at blog composing – don't misunderstand me, they are extraordinary.

Be that as it may, they have another enchantment projectile in their weapons store – they are specialists at infusing copywriting mysteries in their online journals.

They are utilizing all subtle strategies to convince you to peruse, share, buy-in or purchase – without you in any event, seeing it.

With the steady interest for greater quality content and the developing requirement for successful copywriting - one to draw in guests, the other to change over them to leads and clients - reliably creating incredible, a top-notch duplicate is extreme.

Copywriting is tied in with writing to get results (deals, memberships, clicks, referrals and so on). You have to comprehend that the Ultimate point of a marketing specialist is to convince you to purchase what the person in question is selling.

To assist you with maintaining a strategic distance from burnout, beat a temporarily uncooperative mind, and at last get more outcomes, here are copywriting tips from the absolute most noteworthy marketing specialists and publicists.

Compose content with "You"

You can barely handle it, however, I simply recouped from an awful slip-up on this blog. I read a Popular Health Magazine last Tuesday and found how "You" was utilized a few times in the content.

I didn't have the foggiest idea why I read the whole included post, yet at last, the writer said she caught my consideration with "You."

Do you need individuals to feel comfortable when they're perusing your blog entries, articles, and other content types? At that point quit utilizing "we" and be close to home.

At the point when you use "you," it'd send a solid sign that you're really conversing with one individual. You examined, plunked down for a considerable length of time to compose for that unique individual. Since you ought to keep in touch with one individual.

In the event that you need potential clients to walk additional miles with you, address them with affection.

Indeed, utilizing 'you' symbolizes you love them. I may not demonstrate this, however I felt cherished as I was perusing the Health Magazine. Think about why you clicked my title? Since I included "you."

The most significant word in copywriting is YOU. As a blogger, you ought to utilize it ALL THE TIME.

- Get to realize your reader well – what keeps them up around evening time?
- Address them legitimately in your posts (Like I am doing here)
- Be accommodating – don't attempt to dazzle them, and don't attempt to imbecilic it down either.

Go over your last post once more, do you see a great deal of 'yous'? Or then again is the content centered around you as 'Is'

Start Off with Good Headlines

What is the primary thing any reader will see in any article? The feature! To urge the reader to peruse on, your feature must be sufficiently infectious to inspire further perusing. Similarly, as with sentences, keep your feature sufficiently short (ideally seven words or less) so the reader can make sense of what it's about upon first perusing.

There are numerous ways you can bait the readers on. You may utilize a clever feature or something that arouses interest. The most widely recognized (and maybe even idiot-proof) technique is to express the advantage. All things considered, according to #3, anybody perusing the article is thinking about 'how might this benefit me'. Having the advantage uncovered right from the beginning would prod anybody to peruse on insofar as it's what the readers need. Such features are direct to the point and clear to Internet readers, which we as a whole know from point #2, are 'whimsical disapproved' people.

Making it Conversational

Not at all like different types of works like news composing or books, copywriting will, in general, get increasingly close to home with the reader by causing it to appear to be a discussion. Copywriting for web journals implies that it might be perused by a large number of individuals, yet you should expect that you're composing just to a solitary individual. Why? Since any reader who discovers your post would peruse it by oneself at any one time. The person is shaping that association with what you composed and you would prefer not to break the understanding stream.

That sort of association is particularly essential when you're attempting to convince your reader. You have to 'communicate in' in their language and identify with them with individual experience, perceptions, and so forth. Feelings are one of a kind to us people, so make certain to add them to your works too. Different methods for keeping up the discussion like climate are to have short sections and point of confinement one plan to everyone. This guarantees the progression of the 'discussion' stays solid and thoughts remain absorbable and intelligible.

Recount to a story, source of inspiration

I may not be great at a few abilities, yet narrating is my diversion. I took in this from my mother when I was remaining with her years back.

Blog copywriting is tied in with utilizing genuine stories to teach potential clients.

Powerful advertising was started in the Stone Age, where fables (customary stories) was the request for the day.

Try not to compose content that doesn't associate or provoke minds. A short story that addresses the spirit can convince blog readers to act at the present time. When you can connect with an attentive story, a source of inspiration in a split second. It works!

I'm persuaded you to read through to this point since I utilized stories to a great extent.

I caught your consideration, held your pretty hands and I'm tied in with wrapping everything up. Did you discover an incentive in this post, really? Leave a remark on the off chance that you did.

As is commonly said, "Life is an instructor, the more you live the more you learn." Learn to acknowledge life, your intended interest group, the time they spend perusing your content. It's valuable and inestimable.

Keep in mind, you didn't pay them to peruse and share your content; they outed of their own will.

Regard that benefit, and use stories to pass on your message.

State more with less

Long-structure content believers. Be that as it may, long-structure doesn't mean endless content.

Being succinct inside the content is key when composing long-structure pieces.

We've just settled that individuals don't have long capacities to focus. Furthermore, the unquestionably would prefer not to filter through your blog entry to discover the data they need.

Including filler duplicate or unactionable composition to make it increasingly "long-structure" will just irritate your readers.

Individuals will see directly through your cushion and filler.

Try not to be smart.

As authors and content advertisers, we like to play with our words. Now and again that is alright, contingent upon your image character and the kind of content. However, more often than not, being clear and succinct will return more noteworthy prizes than being smart.

As million-dollar marketing specialist Gary Bencivenga stated:

"Successful copywriting is persuasiveness in print, not shrewd wordsmithing. The more self-destroying and undetectable your selling SK."

Some of the instant copywriting tips are as follows:

Cut "that" out

I can generally recognize an amateurish author by the tedious and superfluous utilization of "this," "that," and "these." A particular annoyance of mine is discovering them as the primary expression of the sentence.

At the point when you audit your drafts, evacuate each occurrence of these (that) you can. Follow?

Separate long sentences

Long sentences risk losing your reader. At the point when you put a few thoughts in a single sentence, split them up into independent sentences. In the event that you recognize a comma-substantial sentence, attempt to give every thought its very own sentence.

Decrease redundancies

Arrive at the point by dodging redundancies, for example, "fierce blast" or "new apprentice."

Lose the nothing phrases

"So as to... " and "obviously" are two instances of normal expressions that add nothing to your story. Discover phrases that are essentially filler and hatchet them.

"very" and "truly"

"Very" and "truly" are actually quite futile words.

Cleanse the passive voice

Your composing gets dull when you utilize passive expressions, for example, "It gets known to me." Go with a functioning voice. "I found... "

Use control action words

First drafts will, in general, incorporate numerous weak action words. Make it a point to supplant regular action words, for example, "get" with not so much normal but rather more dominant action words, for example, "seize" or "order."

Take a gander at my promise decision above. "Use" is unsurprising and exhausting. Would "Pick" or "Utilize" or "Apply" siphoned up the exposition? Notice each subhead in this rundown starts with an activity.

Allude to individuals as "who"

Barry is the person that can assist you with your altering. "Who" is the means by which you allude to somebody. Redress: Barry is "who" you have to assist you with your altering. Improvement: Barry will assist you with your altering.

Stay away from the "today stamp"

"As of now" is a stinker. "These days" is as well. Beginning with "Today" or "In today's... " are different useless toss aways.

Wipeout "there is" or "there are" toward the start of sentences

There are loads of approaches to begin your sentences more strangely than "there is" or "there are." Start your sentences with a blast.

We should get amicable

Let us become companions. We should become companions. How about we get well disposed of. I accept constrictions make you are composing all the more neighborly and recognizable. What's more, obviously, striking types of "be" will, in general, liven up the duplicate.

Avoid the - ing trap

"We were beginning to ... " Whenever you see an "ing" in your duplicate, you can most likely improve the line. "We began" is an all the more energizing approach to begin.

Strategies, techniques and best practices to write your content

Everybody needs to distribute incredible content that produces traffic, supports leads, gains interfaces and gets shared on social. Also, why not? Content is as significant as the plan and feel of your site since it drives web search tool results, expands traffic to your page and sets up your association as an industry head. Also, in the present content commercial center, both quality and amount decide your capacity to use content for business results.

Compelling content composing is basic in transforming site guests into fulfilled clients. It's not just about getting content out there—it's additionally critical to delivering great content. Web crawlers creep site content and prize sites with elegantly composed articles by positioning them higher in list items.

In a universe of moment availability, where everybody is, basically, a distributor, the nature of your content regularly seems to be the absolute most significant impression that perusers have of you or your business.

Accelerating the way toward making content (while ensuring all capabilities in a composing group are utilized) and elevating the nature of your content are not totally unrelated. Everything necessary is great arranging, a touch of structure – and this guide for best practice content composition. Having some good times doesn't hurt either. By utilizing this best practice content composing guide anybody can benefit from a quicker pace of yield, better quality, and higher readership. This best practice content composing guide is separated into eight procedures/methods or practices:

Strategy #1: Map Your Audience Personas

As per the Content Marketing Institute, "the main way we can keep up long haul achievement is to persistently draw in individuals." But, before you can do that adequately, you must know your clients. The procedure resembles taking a snippet of data and transforming it into a vital arrangement.

You have to make crowd or client personas, so as to viably overcome any issues between where your crowd is and what you do as an entrepreneur with the goal that your message is applicable.

One approach to begin building crowd personas is to truly give your personas singular names – John, Mary, Timothy, Jane.

Naming your personas, in any case, is just the initial step of recognizing who these people and entrepreneurs are. Next, you must give them socioeconomics and a foundation: how old they are, the place they originated from, where they'd prefer to travel, what their occupation is, and so on. Utilize the crude information from whatever source you approach –, for example, overviews, catchphrase and search term examination and discussion strings.

When planning personas, incorporate whether this persona speaks to your essential or optional crowds. Likewise, incorporate the persona's objectives and how the individual in question may meet those objectives. That data tells you the best way to reach and convince your crowd successfully. Include an image, socioeconomics and convincing duplicate, so you can make your message increasingly close to home, similar to the accompanying model:

Entrepreneurs and organizations of all sizes are grasping and creating purchaser personas since it gives them an edge over their opposition.

Building up a persona can be as straightforward as filling in the spaces of a format, similar to the one beneath. Simply recall that the explanation that you're doing this is to assist you with passing on your message better and to address your crowd's inquiries all the more obviously.

You can send a review or poll or, legitimately request input by means of your email autoresponder (Aweber, Getresponse, and so on.),

At the point when you get input from your intended interest group, assess it against the subtleties of the persona you created. At that point, join the persona into your showcasing methodology. Your advertising effort will yield a better yield, because of this procedure.

Strategy #2 Dynamics

The best online content essayists can ace a wide-scope of composing styles.

Why's that?

Content composing ventures come in all shapes and sizes.

New Media Services summarizes it well.

A few instances of online content structures and their

individual styles are:

News: Short and compact passages, including the outline of the story close to the highest point of the content piece.

Blogging: Friendly, welcoming and stubborn. See any of the posts on the Write Blog for instance.

White papers: Long-structure while giving an answer for an issue.

Contextual investigations: inside and out data giving important information dependent on the research of a specific situation.

Advertisement duplicate: Concise and persuading with the objective of expanding the change rate. Parchment Facebook on some random day and will undoubtedly observe advertisements on the correct board. Here's a case of a promotion from an expert that makes millions utilizing advertisements.

Digital book: A ground-breaking promoting instrument, which can be offered allowed to help email supporters or sold as an item. Here's a model.

An effective essayist is knowledgeable about these fields.

Through this skill, they can assist organizations with accomplishing explicit objectives with quality content.

Strategy #3 Keyword stuffing is rarely alright

Prior to you even begin to compose content, you have to comprehend what you're expounding on — and you can take out two targets with one shot in the event that you join site design improvement with your article schedule arranging. New York Times Bestselling creator and top advertiser Neil Patel calls catchphrase explore "the most significant piece of advanced promoting" and "how we hold our ears to the ground," and in light of current circumstances.

Search engine optimization catchphrase examine mentions to you what subjects Google (and your intended interest group) finds applicable.

Illuminating the content strategy of the competitors and highlighting the strength and weaknesses by your own. It significantly allows the optimization of each article and the content strategy as a whole for bringing in more traffic to the site. In terms of making your content valued, able to to be read and search-friendly, using keywords is the way to do so. But, the cramming of keywords, you might experience an entirely different result.

A web page with unlimited use of keywords tends to be dubious and lacks trust for both the readers as well as Google. This might result in a decline in the conversion and the rankings of SERPs. Extensive use of keywords serves as a low-quality product near readers and they might bounce to another website with no waste of time leading to slap down of your domain.

Strategy #4 Keep the activity in your content composing.

Composing for the web ought to be ground-breaking, direct and punchy. To do that, your sentence structure, word decision, and style need to underscore activity.

For instance, how about we take the normal composing tip,

"don't utilize the latent voice."

The detached voice happens when you switch the subject and item in a sentence. Rather than "the lion assaulted the town" you have "the town was assaulted by a lion."

Notice how the subsequent sentence in some way or another less energizing (despite the fact that it contains an amazing lion?) That's on the grounds that the dynamic voice stresses the activity with "the lion assaulted." In the detached voice, the town is the subject. The operator (the lion that played out the activity) is just referenced subsequently utilizing the prepositional expression "by the lion." It's very nearly a bit of hindsight.

As a web content essayist, you ought to likewise utilize one of a kind and energizing action words to affect the peruser. Have a go at swapping out "deals moved" for "deals soared." Instead of "we cut costs" attempt "we sliced expenses."

Strategy #5 Consistent

Consistency is required by each and every successful writer to stay active on the web. The implementation of such consistency can significantly be done through two different methods.

Voice – It is the source of defining you and your brand. Keep consistency in your voice is considered important in successful content writing.

Your ability of the development of the right voice is based on the period after doing research on your audience and topic. Your popularity among your audience is primarily dependent on your approach towards them and the tone of the content. It is needed to be professional but comforting, if you already have so, stick to it.

Posts – Consistent posting of the quality content, the probability of grabbing the attention of the readers is expected to increase.

A famous tool for online marketing for building awareness of the brand is by means of using blogs. Consistent feeding of content on the web is done through posting of blogs assisting readers in finding your site and get to learn more about your plans and offerings. Additionally, the support to your brand and the creation of authenticity is also promoted by the blog. Factually, in the past year, an approximate of 65 percent of marketers planned significant growth in their blogging use.

Focus – Whatever your actions are, do not wave them when it is about your focus on the content. With the increase in the competition, it is considered important to be focused on the content. Selecting a small niche and writing about the things regarding it is thought to be a way to success. You do not simply need to hop around with no aim, it might cause you the loss of the readers that you have created.

For instance, suppose your interest in a travel blogger who you might come to discover places from. She might come up with a beautiful and adventurous place that tends to fight with your key interests in life. One day, you might take a visit to her site but end up seeing a beauty blog will definitely blow your mind. This is due to the lack of consistency in the content you create.

Strategy #6 Social Media-Friendly

Social media platforms such as Facebook, Instagram or

Twitter are considered as the tip of the iceberg.

In the case of people not found in using Google as their search engine, they tend to be seen on these platforms. One of the most powerful in digital marketing is the ability to capture the attention on social media.

The effective marketing of the quality of social media tends to uphold the ability to go viral. This is known to increase SERPs and ROI. It significantly results in the generation of a wider number of readers boosting the traffic of the site leading to high rates of conversion.

Shortly, the solid strategy of social media can significantly pave your way to the generation of the content resulting in increased revenues.

The platforms of social media are considered to be a magical tool to help you in a personal connection with your audience.

This personal connection is known for the development of the sense of community. And, with its growth, the subscribers and the ability to provide a response to the specific questions.

Strategy #7 Features versus Benefits

When composing item and service depictions, remember to incorporate the advantages of what you're advertising. What are the benefits you inquire? They are everything the client should understanding by utilizing your item and by and large incorporate feeling.

For instance, rather than simply expressing the materials and shade of a downpour coat, you can include it will keep them dry while looking a la mode. This makes acquiring considerably more luring and legitimate as they can envision precisely what they will understand.

Likewise, you can convey torment focuses that clients might be confronting. Proceeding off the coat model, we could make reference to that they won't need to stress over the landing to work doused any longer or getting their hair failed.

Where your clients are in the purchasing adventure will likewise change how you compose your business duplicate. These are the three phases and how you can alter your duplicate as needs be:

Mindfulness organizes: Customers in this stage are starting to acknowledge they require an answer to an issue. Pose inquiries you accept they're considering torment focuses. This will get them all the more sincerely put resources into your image.

Thought to organize: Some examination has just been finished by the client. They might be thinking about you as of now so add more call to activities.

Choice stage: The client is settling on an official conclusion on whether to buy or not. Tributes, surveys, and contextual analyses can help convert them to the last deal.

Strategy #8 Edit Your Work.

After you have made the first draft, return and think about how you may clean the unpleasant edges of your composition. By and large, composing improves as it experiences a round or two of alters—in any event, when it has been drafted by experienced content makers.

Fluctuating the appearance of a page

The great plan keeps away from the two boundaries of a section of content toward one side of the scale and a page so brimming with various highlights that it diverts the peruser at the other.

At the point when you are composing, keep the accompanying open doors for fluctuating the appearance of a page as a primary concern:

- bullet focuses to outline key focuses will improve coherence, however, you should dodge the undeniable trap of populating your page with a huge number of off-putting specks

- callout boxes are utilized for extraordinary offers, significant data, opening occasions, contact subtleties, etc

- pull-quotes include intrigue, yet should be utilized with alert the same number of individuals discover them diverting

- quotations that are longer than a couple of words can be shown, that is put on a different line, maybe indented or incites or in an alternate text style

- biographies of authors generally set toward the finish of articles

- headers and footers, which can contain valuable data

- captions, pictures are regularly used to 'separate the page' yet a useful inscription will include esteem

space – is it better to have indented passages or a line space between? By and large space on a page that lets the content 'inhale' is increasingly appealing and a guide to lucidness.

In the event that your report will be spread out by a creator, ensure you mention to them what you visualize and talk about the choices with them. On the off chance that you are working in Word or a comparative program, you can shift the vibe of the page yourself, however, decide in favor of alert; such a large number of textual styles and various sizes combined with unwise utilization of intense and italic will deliver a wreck.

At long last, make sure to differ your sentence-style.

Have a go at utilizing short basic sentences get consideration, at that point longer increasingly complex ones to tissue out thoughts. Utilize intriguing action words to feature significant activities, at that point increasingly regular ones for assortment. Indeed, even the passive voice has a spot now and again — such as sharing of background data or highlighting the effectiveness of a specified action.

Such changes are primarily not added in the word count, however, they will make your content composing all the more energizing and locks in.

It is an uncommon essayist who can alter their content proficiently. In book distributing editors and editors are given to clean the content. In an office setting, you can maybe ask an associate or colleague to survey what you have composed, or you can utilize an organization, for example, Wordy.

You can likewise evaluate message on your forthcoming crowd — website specialists and marketeers do this as an issue of schedule. On the off chance that you are a non-local speaker of English, getting a local speaker to audit your work will hurl unbalanced expressing and off-key utilization of words.

Which niches to choose and how

Is it accurate to say that you are an independent essayist who is battling to nail the most rewarding composing specialties in the independent composing space? Likely, you are, since huge numbers of us have been there.

Be that as it may, some independent composing specialties are more gainful than others. It implies that there are better-paying composing gigs in the independent commercial center than you can envision. That is the reason you frequently peruse or hear prepared independent essayists guiding you to locate your independent composing specialty, and restricted down your composing specialty.

In any case, it is fundamental to discover and limit on the grounds that forthcoming customers support procuring independent authors who have practical experience in a specific specialty over a general-all-climate independent essayist.

In any case, you may inquire;

At the point when you're picking a specialty, think about these 3 things:

— It ought to be something you're proficient about OR are eager to get familiar with a ton about.

— It ought to be something that a particular objective customer will need and pay for.

— It ought to be something you're keen on as well as

appreciate expounding on.

I will impart to you the best independent composing specialty that you can pick and begin your independent composing venture.

How to Choose A Profitable Writing Niche?

In straightforward words, it is the proportion of interest to supply is the thing that makes a specialty beneficial.

Be that as it may, this is appropriate just if the interest is higher and supply is lower.

In the event that the inventory is more prominent than the interest, at that point that specialty can be said to be immersed and the gaining potential in that specialty is generally lower.

So you need to search for that composing specialty that has low supply and levels of popularity.

Those are the most beneficial specialty.

In spite of the fact that in a similar specialty pay differs from customers to customers and undertakings to ventures however not unreasonably much.

Another choice to discover whether the composing specialty is productive is to perceive how a lot of cash another consultant in your specialty is getting.

In the event that the compensation is higher, you can pick that independent composing specialty.

Yet, take the assessment of different consultants who are working in that equivalent specialty.

These are the rundown of specialties that the greater part of the independent authors profits from.

As only one out of every odd composing specialty is beneficial so you need to take appropriate measures to discover which specialty is increasingly productive and which are not all that you don't need to burn through your time and vitality to no end.

Book Ghostwriting

This one comes top for me since it is an increasingly rewarding composing work the most lucrative independent composing work than the various composing gigs. Why? Since as the name or title proposes, the essayist isn't getting the kudos for composing the book. The credit goes to the customer who will include his byline as the writer and not the independent essayist.

Therefore, they pay well for each task. Actually, the cost for every professional writer book comes at $30,000 ~$35,000. It is an amazing pay and not a poorly conceived notion since the book you composed has the vibe and message of your customer and not your own. Along these lines, customers will work together with you on the undertaking to ensure your content lines up with their voice.

White Paper

White papers dislike some regular long-structure content like a blog entry rather it is a more advanced content type containing more than 5-10 pages of content.

They are a top to bottom report that shows an issue and arrangement so that it very well may be comprehended by the client.

White papers are the most mainstream in the innovation specialty.

Best of all, you shouldn't be a specialist to compose White papers on the grounds that your wellspring of data and content will be founded on Client Interviews.

You should simply to compose and assemble all the data so that your customers get the outcome that they were searching for.

The Payment in this specialty fluctuates and begins from around $3,000 per venture, here and there significantly higher.

As all the whitepapers are enlightening archives they are likewise a ground-breaking deals tool.

Presently on the off chance that you feel that you ought to have the option to nail this composing specialty, have some experience in light of the fact that the installments are gigantic so it requires astonishing composition from your end as well.

Digital book Writing

Digital books are getting increasingly well known as of late. Furthermore, with digital book deals surpassing $4 billion in the United States alone, all organizations and web proprietors are currently making digital books to develop their email endorser list.

The more well known and propelled it turns into, the higher the rate for a short digital book an exceptional sort of content redesign that is intended to change over site guests to leads and clients. In outcome, blog proprietors are paying independent digital book journalists higher rates to complete their employments.

It is a rewarding composing specialty since advertisers are utilizing digital books to produce leads and furthermore offering them to make automated revenue. Did you know? Some independent scholars are charging from $2,000 for a beginner to compose a short digital book?

Be that as it may, even with the best digital books composing instruments, not every person can make a digital book.

Contextual analyses

Regularly, contextual analyses are an assortment of examples of overcoming adversity from individuals in your industry and utilized primarily in the promoting circle to pull in and increase new clients. This zone of independent composing is so rewarding in itself since a contextual analysis content can undoubtedly persuade possibilities to purchase your item or services.

In any case, you can accumulate most contextual analysis articles through meetings with specialists in your specialty who have teamed up with you on a task. You can likewise get nitty-gritty contextual investigation materials from customers you've worked with, including existing clients. Also, a contextual analysis content is normal to compose and structure, in that it gives the:

- Difficulties your customers confronted.

- Arrangements you gave that bailed them out, and

- Results they accomplished from utilizing your item

Moreover, the finish of your contextual investigation will help possibilities to make a significant inference or settle on positive purchasing choices. Likewise, a contextual analysis shows your capacity — the estimation of the services you can bring to the table. It likewise uncovers how you can support your customers and possibilities make comparative triumphs.

Considering this, contextual investigation independent authors are sought after, and the compensation per venture is phenomenal. In addition, since all organizations and organizations are persistently scanning for approaches to out-play out their rivals, the utilization of contextual analysis articles has gotten unmistakable.

In any case, the energizing part is that entrepreneurs are too occupied to even think about writing it themselves or they don't have the foggiest idea of how to compose convincing contextual analysis articles. That is the place independent contextual investigation journalists prove to be useful. So in the event that you can create surprising contextual investigation pieces, you ought to go for this specialty.

Scholastic Content

As the name recommends it includes composing scholastic content including essential article composing for secondary school understudies to the proposal for Ph.D. understudies.

Indeed, even it includes complex composition from designing also.

The multifaceted nature of this specialty makes this

generally rewarding just as the most gainful composing specialty for an independent author.

As I am a Mechanical specialist keeping in touch with certain reports in this specialty is simple for me as opposed to thinking of some proposal.

So on the off chance that you have a degree or comparable information in some necessary field composing scholarly content will be a simple undertaking for you.

Like in the wake of finding out about the composition and distributing industry I am ready to instruct and teach individual writers and authors to bring home the bacon through composition through this blog.

Essentially, you could obtain the expertise and afterward take a shot at some specialty that you believe is appropriate for you and you have enough information to pull through the activity.

The fundamental bit of leeway I discovered writing in this specialty is that I can show customers my experience to compose building related stuff as I hold a degree in the equivalent.

Also, on the off chance that you have some degree you can show to your customers, at that point it makes simpler for you to get work in that specialty.

Aside from that customers can confide in you with the work.

Web optimization and Online Marketing

As an independent essayist, the majority of the employment bids you'll discover will have you make content for sites.

That can mean blog entries, instructional exercises, top to bottom surveys, and anything in the middle. The objective of that content is quite often to get a parent site more traffic, all gratitude to the enchantment of Search Engine Optimization (SEO).

There are countless sites competing for traffic in various specialties. It shouldn't come as an unexpected that SEO itself is a worthwhile specialty for independent authors. On the off chance that you know the nuts and bolts of SEO and can show individuals how to improve results, at that point a lot of entryways will open for you:

A few instances of employment opportunities for SEO specialists.

The equivalent goes for web-based promoting. Realizing how to advance your business online is an incredible method to build benefits and there is a great deal of showcasing forms that work crosswise over a lot of ventures. Email promoting, for instance, can be an integral asset paying little heed to what kind of business you run. That implies scholars with experience utilizing that sort of hardware can likewise discover a ton of chances.

Of the specialties we've secured up until now, SEO and internet promoting are the absolute 'most straightforward' to break into. This shouldn't imply that they're not fantastically complex fields, however, they center around the sort of information you can learn without anyone else. With a couple of blog entries and bylines under your name, it shouldn't be difficult to land some paying gigs, which makes landing more positions simpler down the line.

Wellbeing and Beauty

There's a major distinction between the wellbeing and excellence ventures on the web. A site that is tied in with giving guidance to a solid eating regimen isn't equivalent to one that spotlights on cosmetics audits, to give a model. Nonetheless, the two fields are at last close to home improvement and dealing with yourself, which is the reason I chose to package them together.

All the more significantly, wellbeing and magnificence are multi-billion dollar businesses with a lot of work openings. To give you a model, here's a posting I found after a brisk quest for wellbeing related gigs on one of my preferred activity sheets:

The depiction of a vocation promotion for a wellbeing author.

How to identify posts topic and how to plan them

Building a site, composing posts, advancing content and dealing with everything else in your business can be chaotic. It can even feel endless now and again. No different, things can go to a pounding stop when you can't make sense of what to expound on.

You're out of thoughts.

All that you might expound on in your specialty.... You as of now have.

Well, at any rate, it feels that way.

Surprisingly more terrible, your readers are expecting reliable contents since that is the thing that you have conveyed before.

You're rowing upstream, and the vessel's going no place. (Here and there, when you quit rowing, it feels like you're going in reverse)

The harder you attempt to fill your schedule with executioner blog subjects, the more terrible it gets.

No blog entries = no webpage traffic = no business = back to the 9-5 corporate pound.

A mental obstacle in the realm of online business can come from numerous things. Perhaps you've depleted your present article schedule, have heaps of posts distributed on your blog and don't have the foggiest idea where to go straight away. Perhaps you're another blogger who isn't sure which points would perform superior to other people.

Whatever the case might be, you need a technique (or four) that will assist you with producing new blog entry thoughts on the fly. That is the thing that this post is going to concentrate on. We'll be going over various strategies you can use to think of new blog points, above all, we should discuss how this all identifies with your content showcasing technique.

On the off chance that you haven't characterized the objectives you need to achieve with content advertising, the absence of an appropriate methodology might be a piece of the motivation behind why you're thinking that it's hard to concoct new thoughts. A content promoting system causes you to interface the objectives you need to achieve in your business with the content you're creating in and outside of your blog. It gives guidance while you fill your article schedule with the entirety of the thoughts you have. What you may not understand is the means by which it can really assist you with thinking of those thoughts.

Picking the correct point to expound on your blog is indispensable in the event that you need to compose a post that draws in your reader.

Surging the decision of theme can set you off course and wind up burning through both your time and that of your reader.

While some of the time the thought for a post hits you and needs little adaption – I locate that many (if not most) times the principal thought that comes to me for a post needs a bit of trim (or marinating) before it's perfect. I will frequently concoct a post thought and wind up advancing it into something that is very unique – however which is a lot more extravagant regarding how intriguing it is.

Technique #1: Talking to Your Audience

It might appear to be basic, however, the best method to discover what issues your audience is having is to ask them straightforwardly. Different techniques in this rundown are successful enough, yet talking straightforwardly to your audience will enable you to see the particular, certifiable issues they're having, not simply issues they may be having. It additionally encourages you to build up an association with them, which is a considerably more significant advantage for have than you may understand.

There are various ways you can approach conversing with your audience. Start on your site. Experience your remarks, and connect with analysts who express their issues or aspirations to you. Solicitation to have a one-on-one talk with them on their terms (Skype, telephone, email, Twitter, and so on.), and use it to ask them what the hardest part about being in your specialty is. Here are a couple of models:

"What's the hardest part about being a picture taker?"

"What's the hardest part of learning photography?"

"What battles would you say you are presently encountering in photography?"

You can likewise set up an exceptional contact structure on your site guests can use to express their issues to you and pose inquiries. Overviews or little surveys will fill in too.

Outside of your site, you can utilize similar inquiries referenced above, and include them in an email in your Welcome autoresponder arrangement for new endorsers just as a communicate email for current supporters. Finally, you can converse with individuals in and outside of your hover via web-based networking media or in discussions.

Technique #2: Ask Quora

In the event that you're a general information nerd, at that point chances are you've known about Quora.

Quora is where you can pose an inquiry and individuals will reply as well as could be expected.

Be that as it may, if it's a Q and A stage, how would you discover points to compose on?

There's really a simple 5 stage process for discovering blog points on Quora;

Stage 1: Make a rundown of terms\keywords related to your specialty

Stage 2: Enter every one of those Copywriting in the Quora search box

Stage 3: Go through the discussion and talks that spring up

Stage 4: Highlight portions of the talk which you believe you could expound on

Stage 5: Write a wonderful blog entry on the content you featured and lounge in your readers' appreciation

Quora for blog entry thoughts

I scanned for the word SEO, and this inquiry sprung up.

I can without much of a stretch compose a guide on the best SEO modules for WordPress.

Additionally, I or you do not need to do a lot many things to research about the blog, many of the plugins are already described in the Quor discussion.

On the other hand, if you are able to see the "Related Questions" on the sidebar, you will find out the most reviewed questions.

What number of winged animals would we say we are slaughtering with this one technique?

Many, I'd state.

Technique #3: Research Keywords

Copywriting inquires about a tool like Google Keyword Planner can assist you with concocting blog entry thoughts. These devices can assist you in seeing how individuals search on the web and what keywords they use so you can improve your features and your blog's general SEO.

The last technique we're going to cover is keyword inquire about. You aren't really searching for Copywriting to target nor are you fundamentally searching for torment focuses. You're basically searching for mainstream points individuals look for in your specialty so you can manufacture a rundown Copywriting that will enable you to think of a conventional measure of blog themes. To do this, we will discuss a couple of various tools. I suggest introducing Keywords Everywhere for Chrome or Firefox for instruments that do exclude search traffic information locally or precisely.

How about we start with Google Keyword Planner. When you sign in to your Google account, you can utilize the instrument to include a primary Copywriting and produce hundreds and even a great many related keywords. Start with an expansive, short-tail Copywriting, and work your way from that point.

You can likewise utilize KWFinder, an extraordinary tool to utilize when you need to perceive how troublesome it is the rank for a specific keyword. This tool comes with its confinements, for example, paying for an enrollment record to perform in excess of five quests. That is alright, in any case, on the grounds that there are two additional tools you can go to discover more Copywriting.

The first is Ubersuggest, a straightforward tool that imitates Google's propose work and develops it. You should simply enter a base Copywriting, for example, your specialty theme, to produce tons of keywords identified with that keyword. In conclusion, you can utilize an instrument called AnswerThePublic to create Copywriting in extraordinary manners, remembering for "who," "what," "why" and "how" groups.

Once more, you're not really discovering explicit issues to understand here. You're just attempting to manufacture a huge rundown of Copywriting you can reference while you conceptualize point thoughts for your editorial.

To start your Copywriting inquire about, you need to scan for keywords you regularly use. Make a rundown of 10-20 Copywriting and longtail keywords (gatherings of 2+ Copywriting) to examine.

Technique #4: Pursue patterns

The procedure is to watch out for general patterns in the online networking space and tail them. This will assist you with getting a general feeling of the sorts of content to post. While it won't be quite certain to your audience, I figure it can even now be useful.

For instance, the top content design presently is video. In our 2018 Social Media Trends report, we called attention to that "video posts have the most elevated normal commitment and double the degree of commitment of other post types on average"2. Additionally, as per our State of Social 2018 report, we found that 85 percent of organizations might want to make more recordings in 2018.

I think it'll be extraordinary to try different things with a couple of recordings if your assets permit and perceive how they perform. You can make straightforward recordings without major spending utilizing instruments like Animoto and Lumen 5.

Technique #5: Gain from your industry peers

This technique is to gain from your industry peers.

Take a gander at the top pages in your industry and see what is working for them. On the off chance that you have a comparative objective audience, what worked for them will probably work for you, as well.

It'll be incredible to go past simply your rivals. Are there different organizations that you respect, which you can gain from? Possibly in light of the fact that they are in a similar space yet aren't your immediate rival. Or on the other hand, maybe their method for advertising impacts you. For instance, I frequently prefer to look at the internet based life profiles of HubSpot, MailChimp, and Airbnb.

Use the tool to gut-check your themes.

When you have subjects as the main priority for blog entries, do some testing: Just in light of the fact that you think the point is intriguing and useful for website improvement doesn't constantly mean it will resound with your audience.

Here on the HubSpot Blogging group, we propose blog subjects and titles close by the motivation behind why we figure they will perform well. Here is a portion of the devices we use to decide whether an edge merits reviewing:

TitleTester: As the name of the instrument recommends, TitleTester enables you to plug diverse title alternatives into its device to examine which has the most elevated clickthrough rate. Utilize this device to test various edges on a subject to see which produces the most intrigue.

Twitter Polls: Ask your devotees to decide in favor of subjects they're generally keen on perusing increasingly about utilizing Twitter Polls. Utilize that information to control your point picking before beginning to compose.

Strategies to build your audience from the very beginning

Have you at any point felt like your blog's audience wasn't developing quick enough?

You're not the only one.

Each blogger has had that feeling.

So what would you be able to do to get it going?

Everything begins with a system concentrated on putting your guests first and I'm going to show you precisely how.

In any case, there's another obstacle to this audience development thing.

Furthermore, that is guaranteeing that those readers hold returning to your blog later on.

In case you're hoping to begin a blog, or you're as of now knee-somewhere down in blogging, you've likely scoured the parts of the bargains looking for ways you can make cash blogging. While there are a lot of alternatives, to truly make cash blogging, you need to guarantee that you hold unflinching and consistent with a specific arrangement of criteria. On the off chance that you can do that, at that point you'll likely prevail in the long haul. Neglect to do that and you'll see your endeavors crash and burn best-case scenario.

Each essayist needs a clan. That to say the least is quite

obvious.

Without a group of people of readers, your words will fail to be noticed — regardless of how significant or propelled they appear. Be that as it may, how would you do it?

Incredible inquiry.

Most journalists battle with this. They "simply need to compose," trusting their sharp exposition will sometime get them picked by a distributor.

And afterward, they think, they'll leave all that showcasing and advancement stuff to them. Those folks. The aces.

All things considered, let me start by first saying that it is anything but a matter of minor karma or possibility. This isn't something that will simply occur. Trust me, I attempted.

Surely, everybody's adventure is exceptional. Be that as it may, most essayists who have manufactured an enormous online audience have done a great deal of very similar things. As I contemplated and applied those equivalent procedures, I was shocked to see comparative outcomes.

Having similar data with many journalists and watching them succeed, I'm presently persuaded it's the standards, not the characters that make this procedure work.

What's more, presently I'm going to impart to you the entire procedure of building an online audience and turning into a genuine author. Since once you know these means, you can gather what appears to be applicable for you and start your very own voyage.

In any case, there are some down to earth tips that can

enable your blog to create, develop and even advance into one of the most visited sites on the Internet.

Start organizing with different bloggers all the time

As the idiom goes:

"It's not about what you know, it's who you know."

The equivalent can be said about blogging.

At the point when you start organizing, you'll notice you get more traffic, offers, and commitment on your blog.

What's more, when you've created solid associations with different bloggers, that is the point at which you can make sense of different methods for helping one another.

Yet, recall – there must be a common advantage.

So how might you start becoming more acquainted with different bloggers in your specialty?

Draw in with different bloggers on informal organizations – This can incorporate sharing others' content and reacting to them in remarks of notices.

Leave accommodating remarks on different sites – This is best done on close to home web journals where the proprietor reacts to remarks. This is a certain fire approach to get saw giving you let anything limited time well enough alone for your remarks and spotlight on leaving supportive remarks.

Become some portion of a flourishing network in your specialty – Online people group is an extraordinary method to interface with different bloggers. From Sub-Reddit's to Facebook Groups and discussions, there's bounty to browse.

Routinely include convincing content.

Not only a few times each month. Week after week. You have to construct a convincing content that pulls in a particular audience.

The more defined niche you would choose depending on the popularity and its review will surely demonstrate the possibility of its success that would be encountered soon. Some of the bloggers are known to do an approximate of five contents each day in a consistent manner for over a year or more until you build your audience.

Syndicate Your Content

Blog syndication is the point at which you put a bit or only a bit of content of your blog to different sites. The fundamental objective is to expand web traffic particularly on the off chance that you have quite recently begun a blog. You have a decision on the best way to syndicate your blog, however on the off chance that you are attempting to advance something like an item, at that point you can syndicate the whole article to give careful data to your reader. There are numerous ways on which you can syndicate the content of your blog, yet the most famous ones are through online life. This incorporates putting a portion of your blog content to LinkedIn and Medium thus substantially more. There are likewise other

Blog Design

Your blog design is a colossal factor with regards to pulling in and expanding your audience. Your design ought to be anything but difficult to utilize and anybody can explore easily. You can do a Peek test to perceive what clients do on your site. Most audiences when they visit your blog need to know the blogger's name and data which is as a rule in the "About" page, so ensure this is unmistakable. Furthermore, the typical menubar ought to be sorted out and the remark segment ought to be anything but difficult to utilize.

Compose For Search Engines In Mind

At the point when you have a blog and your objective is to sell and market your items, Search Engine Optimization (SEO) is extremely valuable. Most bloggers disregard this since it very well may be precarious and some of the time even expensive. Be that as it may, an incredible turnout for web traffic is indicated when you put resources into content advertising. An expansion in search rankings will before long advantage like requests for publicizing and even requests for your items. You should simply conceptualize a few catchphrases that ought to show up in your blog and search for individuals who can discover shrewd approaches to assist you with consolidating these keywords into your blog website. Utilizing a simple site module like Yoast SEO can make this a lot simpler to accumulate a great deal of web traffic.

Use Forums

Besides SEO, utilizing gatherings can be an extraordinary method to expand traffic as you start a blog. You should simply look through questions that are identified with your business point and you can help individuals by noting them and in any event, connecting back to your site in the appropriate response. This technique resembles hitting two winged animals with one stone. You are essentially tending to their inquiries/issues and you are expanding web traffic to your blog simultaneously.

Remarking On Other Blogs

Tragically, numerous individuals utilize the remark area to compose spam remarks, which gives a negative impression to this recommendation when beginning a blog. Be that as it may, in the event that you can give an authentic remark, it is an incredible method to welcome other blog scholars back to your site or blog. For whatever length of time that you are not trying too hard and attacking every one of the remarks areas of the site, gatherings and other blog locales like the specialty you have, you will acquire watchers and make new companions.

Guest Post

Hybrids and coordinated efforts are significant for bloggers. You may figure it would advance challenge, yet it is typically seen as associating and augmenting your system to individuals or bloggers who are in a similar specialty as you. You simply need to locate a significant and tenable site and attempt to connect with them by recommending an applicable blog point. You can compose for nothing at the outset and see from that point how you can begin gaining extra from it.

Add to the top online journals in your specialty

In the event that you need to develop your audience, contributing guest presents on top web journals in your specialty will be incredibly compelling.

Yet, so as to get results that will genuinely move the needle, there is a particular methodology you have to take.

Here's the manner by which you should move toward guest blogging:

Recognize writes in your specialty with a drew in the audience – If you're adding to a blog with no following and no commitment, you're not going to get much in the method for results. Social offers and remarks are great benchmarks to take a gander at.

Associate with the proprietor of the blog before pitching them – This is fundamental. We discussed becoming more acquainted with bloggers before; precisely the same advances apply here. Become more acquainted with the blogger previously and all things considered, your pitch will be effective.

Make your pitch about the blogger and how you'll support them – Most bloggers get an insane measure of pitches from guest bloggers. Peruse this post to discover how to compose the ideal email pitch.

Try not to keep down with regards to composing content – I can comprehend that you might need to keep your best content to distribute without anyone else blog, however in the event that you truly need to receive the benefits of guest blogging, go hard and fast!

Manufacture an email list utilizing your guest posts – Just guest blogging without anyone else will assist you with making mindfulness about you and your blog, yet you can likewise construct your email list. It's as straight forward as connecting to a page with a pick in structure from your creator bio. For explicit advances, look at this post by Sue Anne Dunlevie. We'll additionally speak progressively about building an email list later in this post.

Advance your post like you'd advance one all alone blog – The more viably you advance your guest post, the better. The blogger you've composed the post for will value it and likely be available to you contributing later on.

React to remarks regardless of whether the blog proprietor doesn't – Responding to individuals who leave remarks is an incredible method to get saw and increment commitment later on.

Request that your audience go along with you on informal organizations

Considering the sub-heading over, the next may sound odd however hold on for me:

It's imperative to make reference to that your email rundown will be unquestionably increasingly effective at taking your readers back to your site than web-based social networking.

That's true.

Why?

At the point when somebody taps on your social profile, it's very simple for them to spot something different and not return.

I'm not saying online life is an exercise in futility since it isn't.

I am stating that you ought to organize list building by means of your blog over building your interpersonal organizations by means of your blog (at any rate superficially).

The key here is to present your interpersonal organizations once individuals have joined your email list.

Here are a couple of ways you can do this:

Add a pursue catch to your affirmation page – When somebody affirms their membership to your email list, they'll be sent to an affirmation page. This is an extraordinary chance to include a Facebook Like box, Twitter pursue catch or something different.

Welcome your endorsers inside an invite email – When new supporters join your rundown, they ought to get an invite email mentioning to them what's in store from you. With MailChimp you can send a "last invite email" utilizing a free record that carries out the responsibility, for other email suppliers you may need to include this physically utilizing their automated assistant component. This is as straightforward as requesting that they go along with you on your preferred interpersonal organization.

Make an exceptional email for your automated assistant arrangement – Most email suppliers have the choice to make an automated assistant succession. Like the welcome email, you could include another email later which urges supporters of pursuing your social profiles. How you acquaint this is up with you, you could utilize a "becoming more acquainted with you" type email or simply add it to the following email in your arrangement.

Draw in with your audience

On the off chance that you need your readers to hold returning, you have to connect with them.

When you start connecting with your readers you'll

cultivate a more grounded network encompassing your blog.

So how might you begin?

Be available – Being inaccessible is something frequently done in business, yet it shouldn't be finished with a blog, regardless of whether your blog is a business. Make yourself accessible, beginning with including a contact page for anybody needing to connect. Furthermore, consistently abstain from sending messages to your endorsers from a "no-reply" style email.

React to your readers – The more readers you have, the more troublesome this is nevertheless it's essential to do. Regardless of whether through remarking or messages, reacting to your readers should be finished.

Include readers in your content – This can have an enormous effect. Brian Dean is an incredible case of somebody who does this right. He distributes contextual analyses about readers who have utilized his showcasing systems.

These are only a couple of ways you can begin, yet there are likely much more.

Without a doubt, it very well may be tedious however you'll turn out to be nearer to your readers, make a more grounded network and have an enduring effect.

Over to you

Similarly, as with some other type of advertising, it's imperative to attempt different strategies; not simply depend on one strategy. Recall it's hard to figure out which ones will be best for your blog without evaluating an assortment of approaches.

These systems are incredible approaches to build web traffic to your blog website. You don't generally need to spend a ton to advance your blog. All you need is to endure and grow your system to completely appreciate the advantages of blogging.

Presently you have a lot of strategies you can use to develop your audience and some others you can use to keep your audience returning for a greater amount of your content.

How to write captivating introductions

You may find a lot of many articles regarding how to great headlines. Similarly, you might have heard about the great importance of headlines but there has not been much said about the importance of a great introduction.

For sure, every content writer needs a tempting headline to grab the diverse attention of the reader but supported by any compelling or strong introduction. This is due to the reason that the best headline you have written won't be enough. You might think of it too difficult to make someone click on your article as an important part of your strategy of blogging.

Convincing readers to make them read your article is considered as an art to itself. If you are not capable of doing it well then you might be putting your promoters, leads, subscribers and paid customers down.

You work so hard, write an incredible post to help people out there. You have the expectation to make your audience feel delighted through the implementation of some easy tips.

But, you tweak and polish until and unless you become able to find the best headline. The only purpose is mainly to grab attention and arouse curiosity. As it is powerful and you are happy.

But, then a nagging uncertainty creeps in.

Consider, if the opening of your written content is boring, who would be willing to read it? What if the opening sucks and readers go away without reading the whole content?

Such incidents can paralyze the experience of bloggers.

But, you can do anything you want, you like.

As writers, everyone is fighting against the other to grab the diverse attention of the world.

What we need to do is work damn hard for captivating and maintaining the attention of the readers. We need to mesmerize in order to ignore the email pop up. We need to hypnotize the readers to their attention engaged.

Often, you might feel of it as impossible. You might have the question in your mind on how to keep your reader's interest intact? It is easy than you think.

Every part of the story has its own importance, but no other thing is more important than captivating the reader with one opening sentence.

Now, the only thing you need is the guideline to get you in the right direction of writing an attention-grabbing introduction. Therefore, some of the best examples just to give you inspiration in writing the introduction includes:

Keep your first sentence short.

I like reading as well as writing short sentences. This is because it helps in understanding what the writer is trying to say. There are numerous examples of short sentences that are punchy, readable as well as digestible.

But, it often happens that writers writing in great pressure or stress of writing an introduction which results in long and garbled sentences. It is fine to write long sentences but the problem is that it makes difficult and harder for readers to understand. Readers seek out for an easy but good and selective approach to words and thoughts specifically at the beginning. Leading off the introduction with one or more bite-sized sentences.

Start With A Startling Statistic

It's one of the most established eye-catching techniques in the book, however despite everything it works. Present your content by sharing details that genuinely take your audience's breath away. Best of all, the detail doesn't need to be straightforwardly identified with your industry—you can snatch a measurement on pretty much any theme and locate an exceptional point to associate that detail back to the general story you're attempting to tell.

Did you realize that the primary American film to show a latrine being flushed on screen was Alfred Hitchcock's 1960 mental ghastliness exemplary, Psycho?

Everyone adores random data, and regardless of whether you're a bad-to-the-bone Hitchcock fan, you probably won't have a fabulous time truth above.

This procedure is another intensely viable approach to catch your reader's eye from the beginning. It's likewise one of the most generally utilized presentations in a ton of advertising composing. This bodes well; it builds up the general subject of the piece in a fun manner and offers the reader something smart and paramount.

Be that as it may, the genuine explanation utilizing actualities or measurements as a presentation works is on the grounds that it pushes our enthusiastic catches.

State something bizarre.

Possibly, you might be aware of pieces of advice like creating a hook or grabbing the attention of the reader. You might wonder what kind of content can be created to get attention? There are many things to say but they do not actually be suitable in writing the introduction.

It is important to make sure avoiding repeating the same phrases and say something unique and unusual, unexpected that hit the mind of the reader. If your reader continues reading your second written sentence then you have done a good job. Avoid starting off your blog with some sort of boring and representation of common combination words which might result in the loss of potential readers.

Dispatch by depicting a feeling

You need individuals to feel something with your content, and that is the place depicting feelings that can prove to be useful.

The thought here is to distinguish how your readers feel and get them to state, "This person gets me. What else does he have coming up for me?"

Feelings push your readers to keep perusing.

Simply a few sorts of feelings you may depict include:

- Disappointment

- Fervor

- Profound respect

- Love

- Vulnerability

- Stress

- Want

Most bloggers are as of now making this stride without acknowledging it, and it's in reality significantly simpler to consolidate into your duplicate than it sounds. How about we take a couple of guides to get a smart thought of how to apply this progression.

In Elna Cain's post "How To Do Guest Blogging Right And Grow Your Audience By Leaps And Bounds," she composes:

Is it true that you are overflowing with energy over your new blog?

That is her introduction sentence, and doesn't it make you need to understand more? Obviously, you're energized over your new blog! She gets you, and you need to find out about what she has coming up for bettering your blog.

KEEP IT CLEAR and SIMPLE

The ability to focus on the cutting edge web client goes on for merely seconds. Along these lines, with regards to your blog content, you need a presentation that will work quickly and tell your reader precisely what they're getting. In the event that inside the initial not many lines your reader doesn't have a clue what your post is about or why they should understand it, you're in a tough situation.

USE KEYWORDS THAT SHOW WHAT YOUR POST IS ABOUT.

It is safe to say that you are composing a blog about another improvement in innovation? Name that improvement in advance, and let your reader know why it should matter to them.

Expounding on another bug control concern? Try not to wander on pretty much the various services your business offers in the presentation. Rather, offer a reasonable, compact take a gander at the service you're clarifying in this post.

NO VAGUE INTRODUCTIONS.

At the point when you were in primary school, your educator likely disclosed to you that the presentation is for mentioning to your readers what your paper or article is about. That standard still applies.

Your introduction ought to never misdirect, do not have a heading, or make bogus vows to your reader. In spite of the fact that you may keep them perusing for a couple more sections, you may lose them for good when they understand your content doesn't convey.

Or maybe, your presentation ought to unmistakably and briefly disclose what they will get from your post.

Inquire IN ONCE YOU'RE FINISHED.

Did your blog entry go toward a path you didn't anticipate? In the event that you composed your presentation before you composed the body of the post—and numerous scholars do—return and ensure your presentation still corresponds with the content of your post.

Grab THEIR Eye

On the off chance that you don't get your reader's consideration in those initial not many, indispensable sentences, they're not going to stay to see whether you have anything beneficial to state. Consider it from the point of view of your optimal reader. What will speak to them? How could your acquaintance persuade them to continue onward and see what else you need to state?

Here are a couple of straightforward hacks for promptly catching the eye of your readers:

Pose an inquiry. This could be a facetious inquiry aimed at your audience or one that will be addressed later in your post. In either case, questions set the desire for the appropriate responses you'll uncover later in your blog.

Start with a statement. Driving with an applicable and dazzling statement can rapidly get the wheels turning in your reader's head and make them wonder what you need to state with regards to the statement.

State something disputable or bizarre. Stunning your readers from the beginning can be a very viable approach to snare them in, yet continue with alert.

Offer an astounding actuality. Eventually, your readers are there to get the hang of something. In the event that you can show them something bizarre or energizing before they even traverse your introduction, you're probably going to start a quick intrigue and set your blog entry separated from others on a similar point.

On the off chance that your presentation doesn't give anything fascinating to your readers, you will lose them. The more fascinating your presentation, the all the more willing your readers will be to proceed. (You still with me?)

Produce A CONNECTION

At the point when your reader feels a connection with you, regardless of whether through an amusing, relatable story or a mutual way of life, experience, intrigue, or need, they'll be bound to give a further idea to what you need to state. Making an association with your reader causes them to value your point of view, in any event, when they don't really concur with it. Compose an introduction that gets them and makes them feel just as they're plunking down for a discussion with somebody they identify with and trust.

ADDRESS THE READER.

While some specialized or business web journals may discover the third-individual point of view increasingly fitting, numerous others will find that utilizing a casual "you" to address the reader is progressively successful for commitment. They feel as if they're being addressed legitimately, as opposed to addressing at by a benevolent speaker.

At whatever point you are composing instructive material for others, you need to utilize "you" to such an extent (and as normally) as would be prudent.

I've utilized some variety of the word you in excess of multiple times. Why? Since I'm conversing with you! I need you to know this data. I need you to profit from it.

By underscoring "you" in your article, you show the reader

you are legitimately tending to them and their circumstance and not simply composing a conventional article to the general masses.

Be that as it may, there's another side to this. I ought to allude to myself also. I will likely pass on an individual vibe to this article. All things considered, it's me conversing with you, isn't that so? So it's just characteristic that I would allude to myself as well.

Comprehend THEIR PROBLEMS.

What are the key issues that plague your clients? What acquired them to your blog the primary spot? Be certain you comprehend the agony focuses your clients' experience.

At that point, utilize first experience with giving them you get it and that your blog entry is there to take care of that issue. Associate with them by legitimately referencing the issue. For instance, clients who can't recollect their passwords, a glaring security defect that isn't being tended to fittingly, or a kid who has a typical conduct issue. This persuades readers that you comprehend what they're experiencing and gives them the motivator to peruse on to perceive what arrangements you offer.

Make Some Conflict.

Each association doesn't need to be 100% positive. Indeed, a negative association—one that negates your reader's convictions—can be similarly as viable at getting them to continue perusing as a positive one.

Consider educating readers that they're off-base regarding a regularly held confusion. Acquaint them with a conclusion or viewpoint they may have never considered, or offer an introduction that will produce a prompt enthusiastic reaction. Numerous readers won't have the option to help yet peruse as far as possible!

Keep Personal Information Minimal.

Sharing individual tales can be an incredible method to keep readers intrigued. In any case, continue with an alert: The more close to home you get, the less intrigued they will be.

Consider it: OK rather visit a formula blog that offers a fast look to the formula, or one where the essayist continues endlessly about what the formula intends to them? Recount to your accounts when fitting, however ensure they really enhance your post.

Clarify the significance of the article

When you've clarified what the article is, presently it's an ideal opportunity to clarify why individuals should mind.

Everybody on the Internet moves toward each new snippet of data with a straightforward inquiry: "How might this benefit me?"

On the off chance that you need to compose presentations that snare the reader and help your content turn into a web sensation, you need to ace the craft of clarifying what the reader stands to pick up from the data you are sharing—the advantages.

In what capacity will it advantage your readers' lives? In what manner will it take care of an issue they are confronting? In what capacity will it fix an agony they are feeling?

In the event that you see how to rapidly and productively answer these inquiries, you'll keep your readers stick to your article till the final word.

Playoff their deepest desires

Since you've recognized your reader's issues, construct the energy by playing off their deepest desires. It's alright to prod your readers a piece now. It's tied in with building expectations.

Offer a conversation starter about what your readers may need. Recount to a tale about outcomes fruitful individuals have found before. Give a number to how a lot of time or cash they fantasy about sparing.

There are various approaches to apply this progression, yet it's simpler in the event that I show you a couple of models.

A solid presentation is the establishment of an extraordinary blog entry. On the off chance that you truly need to connect with your audience, make your content increasingly shareable, and above all, get your blog entries read, center first around making an incredible presentation. By acing this craftsmanship, you'll promptly improve as a, progressively viable essayist.

The specialty of enticing your readers

You may believe you're a blogger.

You may consider yourself to be an author.

However, to maneuver your readers into your posts, you have to turn into a clinician.

You have to sneak into the brains of your readers so you

know precisely what they're battling with. You have to comprehend their sentiments of dissatisfaction, stress, and depression.

Composing a decent blog entry implies basically convincing a reader that this post is for him, that you'll share your best exhortation to enable him, to direct him, and solace him.

Also, when you've offered him your best guidance, you just need to beat him senseless to get him to actualize your tips.

Along these lines, please. You can do it. Go compose a tempting opening for your next post!

How to understand your audience

With the extraordinary assorted variety of showcasing styles and methodologies out there, it's anything but difficult to dismiss a portion of the basics intrinsic to each procedure. Practically, just a bunch of standards are fundamental for accomplishment in truly every showcasing system out there. One of the most significant is this: You need to know your audience, all around.

For what reason is it critical to know your audience?

Realizing your audience causes you to make sense of what content and messages individuals care about. When you have a thought of what to state, realizing your audience likewise discloses to you the suitable tone and voice for your message.

Let me put this another way. Have you at any point needed to understand minds?

The most flawlessly awesome showcasing messages make individuals feel like you're guessing what they might be thinking. You can express their agony focuses, difficulties, objectives, and wants so obviously that it feels like you're living in a sweet penthouse loft in their mind.

Envision for a second that you have an issue. It could be any issue whatsoever—possibly you need to get more fit, or perhaps the grout in your restroom tiles is turning out.

Presently envision that the individual you go to for help

precisely verbalizes your concern. They comprehend your convictions, qualities, and frames of mind towards your circumstances. You feel like they get you.

They can depict your concern more unmistakably than you can portray your concern. Everything you can do is gesture along while they talk.

You're most likely going to employ that individual, correct?

Have you at any point heard somebody talk about an open figure (frequently a humorist) and state "he's platitude what individuals need to hear" or "he's not hesitant to express his genuine thoughts."

Do you realize what they're truly saying? "He's platitude the stuff I accept yet don't discuss."

At the point when you know your audience, you can cull the words directly out of your clients' mouths and use it in your promoting.

You can understand minds.

That is all truly dynamic. What really befalls your business when you can understand minds?

You get more leads since individuals feel like you get them

You get more clients since drives feel like you get them

You get more referrals since clients feel like you get them

Detecting a topic?

Transformation rates go up. Online life shares go up. Email opens and snaps go up.

Deals go up.

By what amount? Look at this model, composed by marketing specialist Joanna Wiebe for the site of a recovery facility.

The new informing on this site expanded catch clicks by 400%. It expanded structure entries by 20%, despite the fact that the structure was on an altogether independent page.

That is the thing that happens when you truly know your audience. At the point when you can get inside their heads. Computerized promoting, content showcasing... .all your advertising improves.

The essence of any great advanced showcasing effort is to distinguish the particular qualities of your optimal clients, including geographic, statistic, and psychographic factors.

The more you think about your audience, the more dominant your computerized promoting endeavors will turn into. You don't get those sorts of results from a dubious Musician Methuselah "persona." Let's discussion regarding why numerous purchaser personas are a mix-up—and how you can truly know your audience.

Advantages of Understanding Audiences

At the point when you are talking, you need audience members to comprehend and react well to what you are stating. An audience of people is at least one individual who meets up to tune in to the speaker. Audience individuals might be up close and personal with the speaker or they might be associated with correspondence innovation, for example, PCs or other media. The audience might be little and private or it might be huge and open. A key attribute of open talking circumstances is the inconsistent dispersion of talking time among speakers and audience. For instance, the speaker, for the most part, talks more while the audience tunes in, regularly without posing inquiries or reacting with any input. In certain circumstances, the audience may pose inquiries or react unmistakably by applauding or offering remarks.

Consider YOUR IDEAL READER

Depict your reader. Truly, go snatch a bit of paper and a pen and start jotting. Consider your reader's needs, needs, dreams. Discover what your readers look for. Make them grin. At last, be aware of who is perusing your blog!

Think about your socioeconomics — do you advance to understudies, new and eager moms, business people, web advertisers? Exactly who precisely is perusing what you are putting out there?

Once more, consider your optimal readers. Make their situations pertinent in your life. What do you share for all intents and purposes? How might you make a bond with your readers that says, "we're all in agreement"?

Additionally, consider what YOU would need to peruse as a first-year recruit, another mother, a youthful business visionary or an amateur web advertiser. Put genuine ideas and emotions into it and advance to the individuals who are perusing your blog. They will feel the association, which will make them feel extraordinary and need to return to understand more.

Help yourself out and read Tea Silvestre's "My Ideal Client" poll. It lets you know plainly how to move toward your customers, your readers — and how to become more acquainted with them better.

Leading THOROUGH MARKET RESEARCH

Nobody's brought into the world with the capacity to get audiences and recognize what they need. This information never comes simple – on the off chance that you need to think about your objective customers, you must dive in and do your exploration.

Forbes takes note of this is valid for both SEO procedure and content promoting. In the two cases, explore is the establishment. Jayson DeMers, author and CEO of AudienceBloom told the news source that whether you're concocting a keyword procedure or picking a subject for a long-form bit of composing, in any case, you start by contemplating what themes individuals are keen on.

It takes a ton of research to structure the ideal content plan.

"The underlying foundations of utilizing information in SEO ventures are to a great extent examination centered," DeMers clarified. "Investigation reveals to us where individuals are coming from, what's working and what openings that we can abuse in computerized advertising. Statistical surveying assumes a shockingly comparative job in conventional showcasing, helping you become acquainted with your market, pursue the patterns and decide key needs for your image and market."

Once in a while, all that's needed is as a lot of time to do the starter investigate for your content promoting as it takes to really compose your duplicate. Try not to stress over that. It's fine. It's a piece of the procedure – without strong research, you may begin looking in the wrong place and addressing an audience of people that couldn't care less what you need to state.

Make A QUANTITATIVE SURVEY

You should accumulate more data about your audience than general socioeconomics. In any case, that doesn't mean you will expel socioeconomics, for example, age, sexual orientation, pay level, training, business, and so forth.

To accumulate this data genuinely speedily, you can adopt a quantitative strategy. This exploration strategy is perfect for reviewing an enormous populace of premiums, for example, your current client base or potential market.

The least demanding approach to this exploration is to utilize an online overview. The information is then evaluated, giving you measurable outcomes about your populace.

You will have the option to see general qualities about your intended interest group.

This methodology won't give you explicit knowledge into singular encounters. Rather, it reflects patterns and shared traits among your audience. Tip: SurveyMonkey is an extraordinary looking over the tool.

Direct INTERVIEWS

Meetings are viewed as a subjective research strategy, which digs into inspirations, musings, and even conclusions. It is an approach to become acquainted with your audience on a progressively close to home level.

Since interviews are a tedious procedure, the populace you

research will be littler. By and large, you will focus on 10 to 20 meetings.

Perhaps the least complex approach to subjective research is to lead interviews with a few existing clients and possibilities. The inquiries ought to be set up ahead of time and planned so that they uncover the respondents:

Character qualities.

Purchasing inclinations.

Interests.

Inspirations.

The meeting itself ought to be treated as a discussion. There ought to be a ton of tuning in on your end.

Be mindful so as not to place words into the respondent's mouth. Rather, set aside the effort to enable the individual to get profound into their contemplations.

One strategic suggestion: request that authorization record the discussion. Doing so will guarantee you don't miss significant bits of knowledge. It will likewise enable you to catch the careful words utilized.

On the off chance that you genuinely tune in to these meetings, you will find an abundance of data that you can use to effectively market and offer to your potential clients.

Accumulate DATA ON YOUR CURRENT CUSTOMERS

An extraordinary advance in making sense of who most needs to purchase from you is to recognize who is as of now utilizing your items or services.

When you comprehend the characterizing attributes of your current client base, you can follow more individuals who fit a similar form.

Contingent upon how somebody associates with your business, you may have just a little data about them or a great deal. Try not to add a ton of inquiries to your request or select in the process only for audience investigate purposes. This can pester clients and result in relinquished shopping baskets.

Be that as it may, accumulate whatever data you do have about your current clients into a database you can use to follow patterns and midpoints. A few information focuses you should consider are:

Age: You don't have to get excessively explicit here. It won't probably have any kind of effect whether your normal client is 24 or 27. In any case, knowing which decade of life your clients are in, or their age can be extremely valuable.

Area (and time zone): Where on the planet do your current clients live? Notwithstanding understanding which geographic regions to focus on, this encourages you to make sense of what hours are generally significant for your client support and salespeople to be on the web, and when you should plan your social promotions and presents on guarantee best permeability.

Language: Don't accept your clients to communicate in a similar language you do. What's more, don't accept they communicate in the predominant language of their (or your) current physical area.

Spending influence and examples: How a lot of cash do your present clients need to spend? How would they approach buys in your value class? Do they have explicit money related concerns or inclinations you have to address?

Interests: What do your clients like to do, other than utilizing your items or services? What TV shows do they watch? What different organizations do they connect with?

The phase of life: Are your clients liable to be understudies? Unseasoned parents? Guardians of teenagers? Retirees?

In case you're selling B2B items, your classes will look somewhat changed. You should gather data about the size of organizations that purchase from you, and data about the titles of the individuals who will in general settle on the purchasing choices. It is safe to say that you are advertising to the CEO? The CTO? The social showcasing director? Understanding who inside the organization you have to address is a basic initial phase in creating your image voice.

Look to site and online networking investigation

Things being what they are, the place do you get the entirety of this audience to inquire about data? Web-based life investigation can be an incredible method for filling in the holes in your client examination. They can likewise assist you with understanding who's communicating with your social records, regardless of whether those individuals are not yet clients.

We have full aides on the most proficient method to utilize examination on the entirety of the significant informal organizations:

Facebook investigation control

Twitter examination direct

Pinterest examination direct

Instagram examination control

LinkedIn Analytics manage

YouTube examination direct

Snapchat examination direct

We've likewise got a guide on the most proficient method to utilize Facebook Audience Insights, which can give some truly inside and out data about your current Facebook audience, including what other Facebook pages they like and what sorts of gadgets they use.

Look at the challenge

Since you realize who's now collaborating with your business and purchasing your items or services, it's an ideal opportunity to see who's drawing in with the challenge.

Investigating what your rivals are up to can assist you with addressing some key inquiries: Are your rivals pursuing a similar market portion as you seem to be? Is it true that they are arriving at sections you hadn't thought to consider? How are they situating themselves?

We've arranged a bit by bit control on the best way to do contender look into via web-based networking media that strolls you through the most ideal approaches to utilize social instruments to accumulate contender bits of knowledge.

You won't have the option to get nitty-gritty audience looks into about the individuals connecting with your rivals, however, you'll have the option to get a general feeling of the methodology they're taking and whether it's enabling them to make a commitment on the web. This investigation will assist you with understanding which markets they're focusing on and whether their endeavors seem, by all accounts, to be powerful.

There is insight in taking a gander at whom you are contending with. Not to duplicate them, however, to comprehend what's behind their prosperity. It will assist you with social event thoughts of what to compose.

Keeping an eye on contenders' sites

On the off chance that your opposition is an online business, you can begin with investigating their open customer base and read tributes on their site. On the off chance that they're another blogger, ensure they as of now have enormous readership bases — what are they blogging about that gathers so a lot of consideration? What would you be able to state that the blogger's audience could identify with on your blog?

Systems service with your rivals

Maybe there's an opportunity to coordinate with your rival and become accomplices. All things considered, inquire as to whether you can impart assets to each other and together offer a readership base (through guest posting, for instance). Everybody wins! You each get more readers, traffic as well as customer base while readers get the chance to find new and intriguing perspectives.

Keep in mind, however, that you shouldn't copy your rival's

style. Gain from the individuals who are more effective than you, however, stay yourself. You are one of a kind! Your readers will detect this and return for more when they see that you have an alternate point to work off of with various plans to offer.

Return to your audience explore varying

The consequences of your test may give extra knowledge you didn't have when you initially made your objective market proclamation. Make certain to join any exercises you learn and return to your objective market explanation consistently to ensure it still precisely portrays your most significant potential clients.

Remember that your objective market could change after some time. For instance, route, thinking back to the 1980s, Atari advertised its gaming console to kids.

Today, Atari is focusing on similar individuals who played its games, thinking back to the 1980s—however, those individuals are presently matured 35 and up, and see the Atari brand not as a forefront gaming framework, yet as a nostalgic piece of their youth.

Ensure you remain current with your objective market definition as your items and services advance, and as your audience changes after some time.

What's your optimal reader's name?

Now, you may have gotten your work done from Way #1 as of now.

It's an ideal opportunity to give your readers a face, a name, and a foundation story. See Way #1 for pretending procedures, on the off chance that you need. For whatever length of time that you have somebody to compose for. Be that as it may, not a general reader — as James put it, "You have to compose for Dorothea" or whatever the name you provided for your thought reader, "don't compose for a statistic."

I'm composing for you, my optimal reader who's getting a cerebral pain since you can't make sense of how to write such that will connect with your own readers and fabricate a dependable audience.

Most of the data shared as yet have to do with showcasing.

You need to apply dependable promoting standards to have an incredible SEO or advanced showcasing effort.

While a portion of these standards has advanced after some time, what hasn't changed is that you are as yet showcasing to individuals.

It is popular to discuss the developing customer, however, a decent advertiser ought to likewise be centered around what has stayed unaltered: human impulses, inspirations, wants, and needs.

The more you think about your audience, including your objective clients and key influencers, the more prominent achievement you will accomplish through your computerized showcasing.

An overview of copywriting basics for sales purposes

By definition, copywriting is the composition of ads or exposure materials. Publicists compose such notices and materials to produce leads, deals, or making brand mindfulness. A marketing specialist's activity can comprise of more than composing, be that as it may. It can incorporate research of the item, the contenders, and the purchasers who will see the advertisements. These buyers are known as the intended interest group.

Set of working responsibilities OF A COPYWRITER

Marketing specialists commonly work inside an advertisement office or autonomously as a consultant. Their main responsibility is to work with customers to create thoughts and messages that will deliver powerful commercials to sell items or services. While the workmanship chief in an advertisement organization will manage the visual parts of a battle, for example, fine art, the publicist centers around the composed duplicate. The activity of a marketing specialist is to make messages, mottos, catchphrases, and so on for printed commercials. What's more, they compose duplicate for web-based promoting, radio publicizing, and TV ads.

Being a marketing specialist is about much something beyond composing duplicate. Alongside the inventive procedure, you should likewise have the option to fill in as a feature of a group, direct research, set up together thoughts, and so on.

Pay AND OTHER BENEFITS

These figures are just a guide, as real paces of pay may change, contingent upon the business and where individuals live.

Junior marketing specialists may acquire somewhere in the range of £18,000 and £22,000 every year.

Pay ranges for a middleweight publicist - that is, somebody with at least three years' understanding - might be somewhere in the range of £25,000 and £40,000.

A senior essayist with vital and group obligations may procure up to £70,000, in addition to benefits.

Inventive executives who have won battle grants may acquire around £120,000.

Pay rates will, in general, be higher in London and will change contingent upon the size and notoriety of the office.

Hours and condition

Marketing specialists must be adaptable, as their work is very cutoff time driven. Most work Monday to Friday, despite the fact that the innovative reasoning procedure can mean marketing specialists seldom switch off totally. Work much of the time reaches out into nights and ends of the week. Low maintenance, lasting agreements are elusive. In any case, independent open doors are normal, with numerous inventive publicists working remotely from home.

Albeit fundamental office-based, marketing specialists and craftsmanship executives may embrace look into in open regions, visiting various areas to look for motivation. They may likewise visit customer workplaces. Going to photograph and film shoots and sound account studios are likely with certain offices.

The imaginative condition is regularly extremely casual, with loosened up clothing standards. Be that as it may, copywriting can be an unpleasant and requesting vocation with the expanded challenge to make something genuinely remarkable.

There are no conventional capabilities required for being a marketing specialist. Much like different types of composing, copywriting is law-based and tolerating of varying backgrounds, levels of training, foundation, etc. Be that as it may, having a portion of the abilities beneath will make it a lot simpler for you to create a fruitful duplicate.

Individual characteristics

A publicizing innovative marketing specialist/chief should:

- be profoundly innovative and creative, and inquisitive about customers' items or services

- be talented recorded as a hard copy clear, succinct and syntactically right duplicate

- understand the diverse language styles that intrigue to different objective markets

- have superb relational and relational abilities

- work well in a group and with a scope of inventive

individuals

- be ready to work under tension and oversee outstanding tasks at hand successfully

- be profoundly self-roused and efficient

- be ready to see others' perspectives and accept input

- work inside exacting spending plans

- have an eye for detail

- possess great service, individuals and venture the executives' aptitudes.

English Language Skills

A significant level of English language abilities is an unquestionable requirement. Customers will expect a duplicate that uses the right sentence structure, word decision, comma use, etc. Any marketing specialist should give specific consideration to the accompanying territories:

language structure

accentuation

spelling

There are a lot of free sites to assist you with looking over your abilities if necessary.

An Eye For Detail

Furthermore, to go with English language aptitudes you'll require the capacity to spot mistakes in your own work. You'll be your own editor and duplicate editorial manager.

All duplicate ought to be as mistake-free as conceivable before being sent to the customer.

A Wide Vocabulary

A wide jargon is useful. It's extraordinary to have a wide assortment of words to look over, rather than the equivalent worn-out top choices. Be that as it may, in certain occurrences it is insightful to adhere to the attempted and tried words – when wishing to accomplish an amazing feature for example.

Interest

So as to compose persuading duplicate, you'll need to get some answers concerning the item you're selling. This implies finding its highlights, advantages and remarkable selling focuses. Also, on the off chance that you need to move toward the battle from another point, the more you think about the item the simpler it'll be to discover one.

The Ability To See Different Points Of View

As a marketing specialist, it's crucial to have the option to place yourself in the shoes of the purchaser. You should have the option to convince the client that the item or service you are composing duplicate for is going to profit them.

Research Skills

Realizing how to do research will be generally useful. Having the option to utilize the web will make that procedure snappier and simpler. Having great research abilities likewise applies to your correspondence with the customer. Posing the correct inquiries will enable you to comprehend the item or service back to front, which is imperative in the event that you need to sell it successfully.

Incredible LISTENING SKILLS

It is fundamental that you can tune in to your customers and give what they need. They will give a brief and they anticipate that you should tail it. These aptitudes will likewise help when doing your item research and finding the best point to compose your duplicate from.

An Understanding Of User Experience

The best publicists are not worried about the subject and SEO; they care about the client's understanding. Neil Patel at Content Marketing Institute says this is one of the most basic copywriting aptitudes to refine.

Truth be told, he even says a publicist doesn't have to stress themselves with SEO, CRO or UXD.

As indicated by Patel, scholars should concentrate on the client. They can do this by:

Utilizing catchphrases that attention on the client's needs, not the web index.

Make features dependent on what the client is searching for.

Tailor the content to the necessities and perusing limit of the reader.

The Ability To Create Something New, Even If It's Old

Publicist abilities are continually changing depending on

the requests of web indexes and web clients, yet there is one aptitude that will never show signs of change: a marketing specialist has to make something new.

Perhaps the greatest test authors have today is concocting something new. It no doubt has been done, attempted, and reiterated multiple times on the web as of now, and attempting to break out and accomplish something surprising can make some genuine an inability to write.

You may wind up stuck when the task is a theme you're new to or when you're left with an exhausting industry.

For instance, how would you make oil changes fun and energizing? Dislike customers out there are kicking the bucket to find out about their motor's oil, and most don't have a clue what kind of oil is in their vehicle. Things being what they are, how are you going to compose something new, fun, and connecting with when a large portion of your audience couldn't care less?

Tapa Ngum at Lifehack thought of an incredible post on the most proficient method to produce more thoughts, and it tends to be applied to copywriting easily.

Outstanding Research Skills

A marketing specialist must have plenty of assets available to them. While a dominant part of your examination will originate from the web, you ought to likewise be happy to fiddle with print (for example magazines, reference books, books, and so on.).

In case you've doled out a point, you should know precisely where to proceed to jump into the assets for answers.

No, you needn't bother with a photographic memory here. You simply need the capacity to discover answers.

Being web astute is a beginning. Expertise to look for things on Google appropriately, what catchphrases to strike, and how to capitalize on your outcomes. Internet searcher Land recommends continually refining your inquiry after the underlying one is finished with the goal that you can limit the outcomes significantly more.

Above all, you need definitive destinations. With more web journals and sites springing up on the Internet, you can't refer to your sources from just anybody. You have to guarantee the organization or individual you reference comprehends what they are discussing, has sound research, and they are an expert in the business.

We propose downloading and introducing the Moz toolbar. It's free, and it lets you inspect the area authority (DA) of a site.

What's a decent DA to use for your references?

As indicated by SEO Pressor, a DA of 40 to 50 is normal, while a score of 50 to 60 is great, and anything more than 60 is fantastic. Normally, the more like 100 you get, the more legitimate the site/asset will be.

The Difference Between Copywriting And Content Writing

Regularly, the term copywriting is utilized to outline everything identified with content creation with regards to internet advertising. Be that as it may, this speculation isn't completely right since whether a marketing specialist or a content author is utilized relies upon the assignment and the target.

The previous spends significant time in making short copywriting writings with a reasonable message. The standards of the AIDA model are utilized, and the writings, for the most part, have the objective of getting the reader to play out a particular activity. Content journalists, then again, represent considerable authority in making writings with content-related included worth which, when fundamental, can be adjusted to the necessities of SEO.

Be that as it may, this obscuring of the terms content composition and copywriting has not emerged by chance in light of the fact that the two zones are combining. The explanation behind this is as basic as it is conceivable: Content without "duplicate" barely works online anymore. An article may well depict the advantages of an item or service, yet in the event that the feature and presentation are exhausting if the content is a poor elaborate counterpart for the intended interest group, or on the off chance that it is basically excessively long, it won't be especially successful. At any rate from a web-based showcasing perspective, it will most likely neglect to accomplish its motivation. In this way, it is currently important to join an intriguing content with a fascinating introduction.

It ought to be noticed, the statement that "Content is nothing without duplicate" additionally works backward. A promoting message without great content is probably not going to have a lot of effects. In any case, numerous clients have (reasonably) become exceptionally careful about the utilization of empty expressions that don't specify the genuine advantages of the publicized item. Content and structure ought to be brought together to augment the effect of a publicizing effort.

GETTING IN

Around 1,100 office imaginative marketing specialists are utilized in the UK. A lot more work on an independent premise. While these figures are not explicit to the copywriting job, 70% of the all-out publicizing workforce is in London. The following biggest extent is 6.3% in the North West. Bigger offices may utilize upwards of 20 copywriting/workmanship bearing groups. Different places for promoting incorporate Birmingham, Bristol, Edinburgh, Glasgow, Leeds, Newcastle, and Manchester.

The section is exceptionally focused. Huge organizations with in-house showcasing groups regularly utilize publicists to create business-to-business and direct promoting writing. This can be a course in office work.

There are not very many conventional preparing plans, in spite of the fact that offices do offer summer temporary jobs and work situations to certificate understudies. Numerous marketing specialists are procured in an organization with an inventive workmanship chief. Such associations might be shaped by courses. Taking on unpaid arrangements and showing aptitudes is the most widely recognized course in junior positions. Offices anticipate that marketing specialists should display a 'book', or a portfolio, of work that shows proof of innovativeness and development.

The Institute of Practitioners in Advertising (IPA) has a plan enabling understudies to post their CVs on the IPA site (www.ipa.co.uk) among June and September every year. Their Graduate Recruitment Agency Factfile records part offices with organized enlistment programs and is a superb beginning stage for those wishing to make a theoretical way to deal with organizations.

Passage FOR YOUNG PEOPLE

There are no set passage prerequisites. In any case, numerous participants have an HND, Foundation degree or degree in promoting or structure. Different regions, for example, news coverage, promoting, media or English can be similarly helpful.

Innovative capacity is indispensable for this activity and inventive executives might be quick to support gifted scholars from any scholastic foundation. A candidate's arrangement of work might be as significant as their capabilities.

Section prerequisites to these courses shift, however, least passage necessities are normally:

HNCs/HNDs - one A level/two H reviews in important subjects, or a BTEC national confirmation/endorsement in a pertinent subject, in addition to a portfolio.

Establishment degree - three GCSEs/S reviews (A-C/1-3) and one A level/H evaluation or comparable.

Degree - five GCSEs/S reviews (A-C/1-3) and two A levels/three H evaluations, or equal qualifications. There are postgraduate degrees and recognitions in promoting. The passage is for the most part with a first degree.

The Design and Art Directors Association (D&AD) runs publicizing workshops, which can be a method for creating aptitudes, meeting similarly invested individuals and making helpful contacts. These are held in London, Leeds, Manchester, Glasgow, and Edinburgh. See www.dandad.org for dates and further subtleties.

Section FOR ADULTS

This field is overwhelmed by youngsters, with about half (47%) of the workforce matured beneath 34. Some journalistic experience may support grown-up participants.

Develop understudies might be acknowledged onto workmanship and configuration courses without the standard section capabilities in the event that they have a decent arrangement of craftsmanship and configuration work. They may get ready for advanced education courses by taking an Access course.

Training

Beginning preparing is probably going to be in-house direction from increasingly experienced associates and learning at work. Going to outer courses and workshops is normally energized.

A few offices may expect participants to take the IPA Foundation Certificate, which is a web-based adapting course coming full circle in a two-hour test. This is intended to give a review of publicizing and the particular jobs inside the business.

All individuals utilized in this field will be relied upon to stay up with the latest with industry patterns and gauges by perusing pertinent productions.

Jumping ON

Junior marketing specialists might be elevated to 'middleweight' and afterward senior 'heavyweight' publicist positions. To arrive at the situation of inventive chief, marketing specialists normally need in any event five to ten years experience dealing with prominent publicizing efforts and some industry grants. Publicists will regularly move with their promoting craftsmanship chief accomplice.

Those working in littler offices may need to move areas and managers to advance. Numerous fruitful marketing specialists move into independent work, either sourcing their own customer rundown or joining organizations that spot publicists and media experts. There might be some abroad chances, especially for marketing specialists talented recorded as a hard copy for explicit industry divisions, for example, IT, broadcast communications or fund.

The Best Tip You'll Ever Receive

There's one tip we can give you that will make a beginning as a publicist that a lot simpler. It's ostensibly the best tip you'll get. Here's the reason. You're by all account not the only individual who imagines that possibly they'd prefer to turn into a marketing specialist. Truth be told, tons of individuals think something very similar consistently, however, most never make it past composing articles for a couple of bucks each.

The explanation is this.

A marketing specialist is a sales rep who sells utilizing the composed word. Albeit a publicist must be a decent author so as to achieve this present, it's significant for you to understand that your definitive activity is to sell. How incredible your composing is doesn't make a difference if your composing can't sell. All things considered, you should begin to consider yourself a salesman equipped with a console, as opposed to an author furnished with mind and imagination.

At the point when you're a marketing specialist, you are not a fiction author. You are not a writer. Keep the extravagant, cutesy language for those things, and overlook it when you're composing duplicate. The cleverest, adorable advertisements are incredible on the off chance that you need to flaunt how clever you are. Be that as it may, prepare to have your mind blown. They, for the most part, don't carry out their responsibility. They don't sell!

Thus, that is your tip. Be a publicist. Be a sales rep. Try not to be anything less – or attempt to be something more.

How to expand the audience

Indeed, even propelling a site can appear to be overpowering. When you've made sense of the nuts and bolts of setting your blog up, regardless you're left confronting the much more noteworthy test of getting your first readers... and in the long run, developing that considers along with the thousands.

The following test will figure out how to change over those readers into email endorsers, and it'll before long be an ideal opportunity to adapt your audience through an online store, partner programs, advanced items, ads, a help based business or something else.

In the course of recent years, I've developed my blog from only a little side task into turning into a productive site that presently acquires a large number of readers and well more than six-figures inside pay for me every year.

What's more, that isn't a mishap. I've been lucky enough to work for some mind-boggling organizations and (get paid to) build up my very own procedure for making a repeatable content technique that routinely produces new readers for a site. I've effectively applied those equivalent exercises to my own blog, and that is actually what we're covering here today.

We'll begin by covering how to put a reasonable content methodology together, and afterward we'll plunge into the careful strategies I've used to advance my content and produce a large number of readers.

Characterize the objective of your blog.

What's the main reason for making content on your blog? What are you at last wanting to accomplish? Is it to drive traffic and get readers?

To get individuals to pursue your email pamphlet?

To get them to download a book you composed or some other asset?

To produce leads for an item you will make?

This objective may change as you go from figuring out how to begin a blog and move towards concentrating exclusively on developing traffic, yet it's as yet critical to explain your motivation at an early stage.

Comprehend and interface with your readers.

Your readers will decide if your site is effective. So as to compose content that will really support them, you have to genuinely get them. To begin, consider the socioeconomics and psychographics of your optimal audience:

Socioeconomics: The quantitative attributes of your readers. Think, age, sexual orientation, area, work title, and so forth...

Psychographics: The more "unmeasurable" qualities like qualities, interests, mentality, and conviction frameworks.

When you've recorded these attributes for your objective readers, you can concoct an audience of people persona—a fictionalized rendition of your who your readers are.

Gather email supporters

Each online business lives or kicks the bucket by the size and commitment of its email list.

In case you're as of now getting readers, however, don't endeavor to gather their email addresses, it will be hard for you to develop your blog over the long haul.

By your blog, your email list will be the most significant resource you have in your advertising arms stockpile to develop your blog—as far as traffic and income.

For a certain something, you really claim your email list. By building an email rundown of connected fans, you can stress a ton less over Google or Facebook all of a sudden changing their calculations one day, and ending up without a group of people medium-term. It's one of the most long haul, manageable approaches to develop your blog and bring back recurrent readers.

Email isn't simply the most ideal approach to reliably take guests and readers back to your blog—it'll likewise be your essential technique for connecting and speaking with your audience on an individual level. In any event, something as straightforward as a bulletin that gives reports on your most recent content and what you're taking a shot, freely go far towards building that feeling of knowledge, as, and believe that your audience has with you.

Start investigating various strategies to develop your email list, for example, lead magnets, pop-ups and content updates (don't stress, we'll be getting into these somewhat later). Ensure you're likewise dealing with your email list with the privilege blogging tools like ConvertKit (or assess the most elite in my examination of ConvertKit versus

AWeber versus Mailchimp).

Settle on your key content columns.

With regards to picking what you'll expound on your blog, you have to have a couple of center points that will integrate everything. I like to consider these content columns just like the establishment that holds up the remainder of your blog and keeps everything on-topic.

A case of this with a "promoting" blog would have a couple of columns like online networking showcasing strategies, content composition, and advanced publicizing tips that all assistance to keep your blog centered. It additionally gives you a voice you can compose from.

Conceptualize winning content thoughts.

At this point, your content technique should answer who you're composing for and which subjects you'll cover. Be that as it may, shouldn't something be said about the genuine articles you'll compose?

This is the place I accept a straightforward publication schedule is so significant. It's a basic spreadsheet or schedule style archive you can use to round out, relegate distributing dates, and ensure you'll generally recognize what to compose straightaway.

Presently, here's the straightforward procedure I use for concocting article thoughts for my very own blog:

Consider intriguing points, terms and record them all: Start by recording the same number of thoughts or keywords that you can. Focus on things you realize your audience would discover valuable. Is it accurate to say that they are interested in building items and growing a business? At that point utilize your mastery around a subject like-new item improvement to assist them with filling in their own spaces regarding the matter. Draw from your very own understanding as much as you can and it'll be anything but difficult to concoct point thoughts.

Utilize a keyword look into an instrument to assemble many more thoughts: You need a huge amount of blog entry subjects at this stage, so utilize a catchphrase wayfarer device like Ahrefs or Moz to assist you with rounding it out. These devices will give you terms and points identified with the ones you've just concocted, just as how much traffic those terms are getting the opportunity (to show that your audience thinks about them).

Cluster comparative thoughts together: Your rundown ought to be entirely sizable now. So take every one of those terms and begin to refine them. Are there copies that you can lump together? Do some fair not look at this moment? Refine and alter it down.

Put your thoughts in a spreadsheet and organize: Start a spreadsheet and incorporate your catchphrase, assessed search volume, trouble, and chance to help organize every thought. You ought to have the option to get this data from the catchphrase instrument you use. Presently, taking a gander at all these, allocate a need to everyone either on the size of 1-5 or an essential High-Medium-Low.

Framework content that hits each of the three key needs: Take your top needs and set cutoff times for them. Search for points that hit every one of the three key needs: Fits your content columns, are veritable needs of your readers and have some traffic potential.

Since you have a pipeline of content for your blog, how about we talk about advancement.

Advance your content and produce traffic to your blog

What do you really do once you've hit distribute on your blog entries? It's an inquiry I hear over and over from my readers. Here are a couple of the most ideal approaches to begin getting before new readers and keeping them returning for additional.

Utilizing (the right) internet based life stages

One of the first place that turns in to web-based sites of social media networking such as Facebook, Twitter, Instagram, Snapchat, Reddit and LinkedIn are considered to be the best platforms that suits both your niche or audience. This is the right one and needs to be noted.

There's no reason for attempting to advance your blog entries on each internet based life stage. Rather, search for the ones that give you the best return. The key thing here is to trial and see what works for you.

This is quite an expansive speculation, however, this is what works best on every social stage:

Facebook: Videos and curated content

Instagram: High-res photographs, statements, and Stories

Twitter: News, blog entries, and GIFs

LinkedIn: Professional content and vocation news (local video functions admirably here)

Pinterest: Infographics, bit by bit photograph guides, visual content

Google+: Blog presents you need on rank well on Google

Reddit: Comments about themes in your specialty

Distinguish influencers and increasingly settled brands that normally share content like yours on their social channels. Work to fabricate associations with them, offer some incentive through citing them in your blog content, and label them when you share that content with your social audiences.

Arrangement a member showcasing plan to draw in your audience and convert uninvolved readers into dynamic shoppers.

After some time you'll have the option to stand out enough to be noticed, and in the long run, you can inquire as to whether they'd be keen on sharing your content (in this manner expanding your scope) or working together in different ways.

In the event that you have a financial limit, you could likewise choose to put advertisements on, for example, Facebook or Google to advance your blog. Facebook offers the alternative to help your post, ensuring it'll get more exposure.s

Facebook really enables you to truly concentrate on the statistic you might want to reach with settings for age gathering, area, and interests, making it very simple to focus on your ideal audience.

Guest posting for different web journals in your industry

Perhaps the best thing about blogging, is that there are as of now other increasingly settled bloggers expounding on the equivalent (or comparable) subjects. Furthermore, guest presenting on those significant web journals is perhaps the most ideal approaches to associate with a previously existing audience.

At the point when I initially began my blog, it was principally about outsourcing. I started pitching guest posts practically immediately on related themes like how to structure an independent agreement that will get you paid on schedule and the strategies I use to be progressively profitable as a specialist. I'd make spreadsheets and contact editors or the proprietors of sites about outsourcing and side hustling.

It required some investment to pick up footing, yet it turned out to be a lot simpler as I got distributed somewhere else. Start by following moderately little sites with connected audiences and industry productions with a comparable audience to the one you need to fabricate.

It might appear to be a great deal of work, yet those early guest posts will assist you with building your own audience. What's more, in the long run, as your system develops, you'll have the option to make more associations and post to significantly progressively trustworthy web journals.

Building traffic to your blog is driven fundamentally by getting before (and drawing in) your optimal readers in the different goals they effectively visit on the web. What's more, in this guide on my blog, I plunge into many more techniques I've used to achieve that objective.

Be Personal, Be Unique, Share The Journey

It's essential to build up a one of a kind voice. Individuals relate well to others so build up the propensity for utilizing the words "I" and "me" instead of "we" or "us" which are less close to home.

As indicated by Neilson inquire about, customers trust 92% of suggestions from "individuals I know" however just 37% trust search advertisements and just 24% trust online standard promotions.

Trust is the reason for building a long haul association with blog readers, so try to write in the principal individual.

Other than being close to home and building up a credible voice, you ought to endeavor to build up a one of a kind point that makes your content interesting AND one that makes your audience feel like they are in the interest of personal entertainment with you as you develop after some time.

The best case of this is the GrooveHQ blog where they transparently share their income numbers with their audience.

Effortlessness IS THE KEY TO BRILLIANCE"

That is one of my preferred Bruce Lee statements (did you realize he was really a thinker?).

The more intelligence I gain the more the possibility of straightforwardness gives off an impression of being generally valid.

Simply look at which PC organization is the move adored, generally regarded, and generally beneficial: Apple.

Be that as it may, don't misjudge. For Apple's situation, Steve Jobs was fixated on straightforwardness as an approach to improve the general ease of use and client experience.

You ought to embrace a comparative outlook with regards to your blog and web architecture too.

A basic, clear plan will ordinarily prevail over an intricate structure.

How would I know this? Since Google — with is gigantic userbase and pool of assets – chose to lead an investigation of this very question.

They saw that clients made a decision about a site as excellent or not inside a part (1/50th – 1/20) of a moment of landing on the page. The examination additionally saw that clients found more straightforward plans as increasingly lovely.

Cooperate WITH OTHERS TO "Take" THEIR TRAFFIC

The best exercise of development I can give you is this: to get the chance to scale expand over what as of now has scale.

Search engine optimization and web-based life work of this equivalent guideline since you're exploiting the size and size of Google or Twitter's huge client base.

Be that as it may, social and search are just 2 pegs in a 3 legged stool.

The leg is organizations, which can incorporate (however isn't constrained to) joining forces around another person's email rundown or composing a guest blog entry.

The thought is that the proprietor of the benefit (for example the email list and additionally site) will get great content (and in case you're selling something, an associate commission).

Here are the absolute most mainstream instances of this.

Traffic Genesis – The business people behind this Facebook promoting information item adroitly banded together with at any rate 4 other surely understood advertisers for this dispatch. Since I'm bought into their email list just as the email arrangements of their 4 accomplices, I got the chance to perceive how this played out. For example, Eben Pagen (one of their dispatch accomplices) sent me an email discussing the "new" way savvy advertisers are getting traffic which incorporated a connect to the Traffic Genesis point of arrival.

Support is popular for having developed to a run pace of $80,000 every month (totally bootstrapped) by building their traffic and client base off the rear of a forceful guest blogging technique. Bryan Harris over at VideoFruit.com likewise archived how he had the option to develop his email list 358% quicker (procuring 523 email pick ins versus the ordinary 114 for the week) by guest posting on various online journals.

On a progressively close to home level, I have one companion (who will stay mysterious) who as of late developed his email list by 3,000 new endorsers just from facilitating 1 online course which was advanced through an accomplice site's email list. George Kao, the proficient mentor, and a companion, utilized a comparative method to assemble an email rundown of 10,000 endorsers.

Main concern: don't simply make incredible content for yourself, structure the propensity for doing it for others too to develop your audience significantly quicker.

Obviously, all the traffic on the planet won't prompt the assurance of a fruitful online business. On the off chance that you need individuals to peruse what you're composing—and intentionally choose to return for additional—you have to give them motivation to.

Compose helpful content, endeavor to contact your audience, truly interface with those readers, and continue offering some incentive to them.

On the off chance that you can do that, the traffic will keep on increasing.

Content promoting through your blog is the best method to fabricate an audience of people at this moment. It doesn't require as a lot of exertion as you would suspect and it gets simpler with time.

Composing ordinary and distributing something new at any rate once every week has enormous advantages for your rankings in web search tools, social sharing, and causes you to structure a strong daily practice

Try not to be bashful about catching email addresses — it's the best method to stay in contact and it's multiple occasions more powerful than imparting however internet based life channels.

It's about the nature of the content, yet about how well you advance it that characterizes your compass and pace of audience development

Keep your structure straightforward.

Be exceptional, individual, and legitimate in what you compose

Google needs to offer it's clients responses to their inquiries. Do your examination so as to use this traffic.

Part with your best content by means of guest posts (however be vital by the way you do it)

For organizations, constructing a hostage, steadfast audience implies you can invest less energy and exertion selling since trust will as of now have been assembled.

How to comply with SEO best practices

Search Engine Optimization (SEO) is the craftsmanship and study of driving focused on traffic to your site from web indexes. Regular undertakings related to SEO incorporate making excellent content, enhancing content around explicit keywords and building backlinks.

As should be obvious, about 60% of all traffic on the web begins with a Google search. Furthermore, on the off chance that you include traffic from other mainstream web crawlers (like Bing, Yahoo, and YouTube), 70.6% of all traffic begins from a web crawler.

Considering this point, when you might look for something in Google, it consistently filters out the best and most relevant results for you.

In particular, Google examines its file of "several billions" of pages so as to locate a lot of results that will best answer your inquiry.

How does Google decide the "best" result?

Despite the fact that Google doesn't make the inward activities of its calculation open, in view of documented licenses and proclamations from Google, we realize that sites and site pages are positioned dependent on:

Significance

On the off chance that you can for "chocolate chip treat plans", you would prefer not to see website pages about truck tires.

That is the reason Google looks as a matter of first importance for pages that are firmly identified with your catchphrase.

In any case, Google doesn't just position "the most significant pages at the top". That is on the grounds that there are thousands (or even a great many) applicable pages for each search term.

Authority

Authority is much the same as it sounds: it's Google's method for deciding whether the content is precise and reliable.

The inquiry is: how does Google know whether a page is legitimate?

Value

The content can be significant and definitive. In any case, if it's not helpful, Google won't have any desire to situate that content at the highest point of the list items.

Truth be told, Google has freely said that there's a qualification between "more excellent content" and "helpful" content.

Site design improvement isn't one single assignment or methodology you execute to support your site to the highest point of web crawler rankings. A viable improvement plan consolidates an assortment of best practices for SEO that meet up to assist sites with picking up an expert in SERPs.

The estimation of appropriate SEO can't be overestimated. Regardless of whether it builds the perceivability and discoverability of business inside web index results, or diminishes the expense per click by improving the page quality score, enhancement is a significant worry for the present organizations.

This extended arrangement of reports considers every one of the parts of SEO. It begins with the basics, including an available explainer on how web search tools decide pertinence in website pages, interprets Google's most huge calculation changes lately and how they influence brands, and thinks about how content chiefs can function with PRs and writers to support their organizations' perceivability on the web.

Content SEO

The craft of content SEO includes making content that is exceptionally viable at noting individuals' hunt inquiries.

At the point when individuals scan for something on the web, they need to discover content that offers them an incredible response to what they are searching for.

On the off chance that your article is the absolute best bit of content that exists on the theme, at that point the web crawlers' refined calculations and AI should begin demonstrating your content in the end.

Another significant piece of content SEO is utilizing your keywords and their equivalent words in better places to ensure that the web crawlers recognize what your content is about.

It is generally imperative to remember your catchphrases for a characteristic path in the title, yet additionally remember them for a characteristic structure in different places inside the content.

Remember that top-notch content is affirmed by Google just like the absolute most significant positioning variable.

Keyword Optimization

When you are content with the quality and length of your content, you'll need to ensure you've incorporated a fitting measure of essential keywords, just as inert semantic ordering (LSI) catchphrases. Essential catchphrases are terms that outline what your content is about. LSI catchphrases are supporting keywords that identify with the essential catchphrases.

For instance, the essential catchphrases of this post are "Search engine optimization best practices," which you will see sprinkled all through. Our objective when you type "Web optimization best practices" into Google is for this post to rank as high in your natural indexed lists as could reasonably be expected. LSI catchphrases incorporate "Website design enhancement systems," "natural hunt," and "Search engine optimization agenda," among others, all of which bolster the essential keyword "Web optimization best practices."

Google perceives LSI keywords and comprehends that they are adding more seats to your content. Hence, LSI catchphrases assist appear With googling that your content is high in quality and ought to be positioned higher on the SERP than other, lower-quality content.

Things being what they are, how frequently would it be advisable for you to utilize your essential keyword? At the very least, we prescribe a catchphrase thickness of 2 to 5 percent.

Monitor your backlinks

Monitoring your backlinks is similarly as significant as building them. That is on the grounds that SEO depends on the nature of the backlinks your site gets. The more top-notch joins you have, the higher you will rank in Google. Building backlinks isn't sufficient. You likewise need to screen each connection your side is winning. Not realizing who connects to you or when connections are being expelled can cost you a ton of traffic. All things considered, nobody would need to be a casualty of negative SEO.

To effectively track your connections, you can again utilize Monitor Backlinks. It enables you to add labels to your site's connections, get email cautions when your site wins another connection or when one of your old ones are being evacuated.

Meta Titles and Meta Descriptions

Meta titles and meta portrayals (meta-information) are the blue connection (meta title) and the section of content (meta depictions) that regularly show up in internet searcher result bits. Meta titles are as yet one of the most significant on-page positioning variables in 2018 - and will be for quite a while.

The depictions don't straightforwardly impact web index rankings, i.e., they are not one of the variables/signals utilized by the Google search calculation. In any case, they are a basic piece of your site's On-Page SEO in that:

They help to depict your site pages to the web indexes, along these lines making your content progressively significant

They go about as natural content for your site pages, and when web crawlers are showing the outcomes, the meta title and meta portrayals will have appeared as an outline of the content found on your web search tools

On the off chance that your meta title and meta depictions are sufficiently convincing, they will expand the active guest clicking percentage of your site, in this manner boosting the natural traffic landing on your sites

In addition, when composing meta titles and meta depictions, you can likewise add modifiers and qualifier words to your keywords and key expressions.

For instance, if your objective catchphrase is a shop, a portion of the modifiers you can utilize incorporate shops, shopping, stores, store, and so on. In addition, you can utilize qualifiers, for example, on the web, purchase, deal, best, modest, reasonable, and so forth.

These additional words in your meta information will expand the focusing of your pages by helping them to meet all requirements for different expressions that individuals might be scanning to discover your items. In this way, elegantly composed meta information is as yet one of the most fundamental SEO factors, and since it improves your natural indexed lists, it will keep being one of the top SEO rehearses in the coming years.

Inside page connecting with stay content

Interior connecting alludes to a connection on a page that

focuses on another page on a similar site. Inside connecting is significant on the grounds that it fortifies those keywords inside for those pages, it permits clients (and internet searcher robots) to explore through the site, and it tells the web indexes that the page is important for that catchphrase expression.

An alt tag is basically the name of a picture. All pictures should utilize suitable alt labels. Not exclusively are alt labels useful for web crawlers; they are likewise useful for availability. In the event that somebody is utilizing a screen reader, they will have the option to hear what that picture is.

You should attempt to incorporate your catchphrase expression for the sake of your picture, if conceivable, however, don't try too hard. Picture file names ought to likewise be SEO neighborly. Picture search is substantially more generally utilized than accepted, so traffic from that point is likewise important.

Broken Links and Duplicate Content

One of the few issues that are at present influencing and will influence internet searcher rankings in 2018 and past issues such as broken connections, malicious connections, copy content, malware, etc.

Luckily, Google has an approach to assist you with staying away from these issues, in this manner keeping up or even lift your internet searcher positioning. This comes as Google Search Console, which was some time ago known as the Google Webmaster Tools.

The Google Search Console is a free device (service) that causes you to screen the wellbeing of your site. With search support, you can screen your site, enabling Google to check it for you and caution you of the issues referenced previously. When setting up the profile, you can include every one of the URLs of your site. Ie, with the www and without the www in the URL just as the HTTPs and HTTP variants.

Along these lines, Google will have the option to screen all the potential forms of your site URL, abstain from punishing you for copy content, and caution you of broken connections and different issues that can influence your site's web crawler rankings.

What's more, Google Search Console can assist you with monitoring your site's web crawler execution by furnishing you with fundamental data, for example,

The inquiry inquiries that prompted your site showing up in query items

Thought of the measure of traffic your site got from each inquiry

Destinations that are connecting back to your site

The web index execution of your versatile website

With this data, you would thus be able to have the option to settle on educated choices concerning your SEO battle, which will, thus, help you to improve its web crawler rankings.

Page Load Speed

Everybody who possesses a site realizes how significant page load speeds are with regards to expanding the change paces of a site. As per a few examinations, clients expect quick page load velocities, and a large portion of them will desert a site in the event that it takes over 3 seconds to stack its pages.

Be that as it may, what a few people don't know is that their very own site stacks up quicker in light of the fact that every one of the pictures is now stored on their machine. Also, on the grounds that page load speeds are one of the numerous elements utilized by Google to rank sites in query items, its value clearing your reserve to show signs of improvement perspective on how the site loads for your forthcoming audience.

A site with poor page load speeds is probably going to experience the ill effects of low change rates, yet in addition poor traffic because of low web search tool rankings. As a site proprietor, improving your site's page load speed is in this manner one of the most significant SEO assignments you should do on the off chance that you wish to show signs of improvement web crawler rankings in 2019.

All in all, how might you improve your site page load speed?

To improve your site page load time, you need to get rid of whatever hinders its presentation. This incorporates substantial pictures (tremendous record estimates because of enormous measurements or print as opposed to web pictures), slow stacking content, an excessive number of modules, too many sidetracks, massive site documents (illustrations, adverts, and so on.), slow servers, and others.

These reasons for moderate burden times can be particularly impeding to your web crawler rankings when they are on your portable site – cell phones have a more slow exhibition contrasted with PCs, and hence clients will encounter even more slow speeds when utilizing cell phones.

With regards to slow page load speeds, you should take note of that internet searcher bots will, in any case, consider your site moderate, regardless of whether you have utilized strategies, for example, program reserving to support your site speeds. This is on the grounds that with program reserving, the site records (pictures, illustrations, a portion of the content, and others) are put away in the client's program store to help the speed of the site when they are visiting it once more. Consequently, as referenced over, the site will, in any case, be delayed for first-time clients or clients who routinely clear their store.

The best arrangement is in this manner to guarantee that the site is totally enhanced to improve the heap speed. Subsequent to upgrading it, you should then test the heap time utilizing instruments, for example, https://www.webpagetest.org, which will assist you with recognizing the genuine burden time of your website and of substantial components that take an age to stack up.

Portable Website

For quite a while now, Google has been centered around making list items progressively pertinent to versatile clients, particularly with the consistently expanding pace of portable traffic to a point where it has outperformed work area traffic. After a few versatile amicable updates to their hunt calculation, Google has at long last concocted the last arrangement – the Mobile-First Index positioning framework.

The Mobile-First Index framework will be one of the most significant internet searcher signals utilized by the web crawler monster to rank sites. As the name recommends, the Mobile-First Index will offer inclination to the versatile form of sites, rather than the present ordering framework utilizes work area variants. The new file framework is intended to offer a superior encounter to most of its clients, who are presently portable clients.

The framework is presently being turned out, and will go into full impact mid-2018. When this occurs, sites that don't have a versatile site or whose work area sites are not responsive will undoubtedly encounter a huge drop in the internet searcher results pages. In this manner, in the event that you don't have a portable site, or your work area site doesn't show up on web indexes when utilizing a cell phone, it is time you start making the essential solutions for agreeing to the Mobile-First Index framework.

Be that as it may, as you are consenting to this new file framework, you should take note that just having a versatile site won't promise you high rankings. For your site to be positioned in the top outcomes, it must be awesome. Hence, a portable site is only the initial step, and you should be in consistence with other Google SEO elements to be positioned profoundly. Truth be told, it is smarter to just have a responsive work area site rather than a low-quality versatile site.

Site Dynamics

Ensure your site is quick, mistake-free, and streamlined for progress. Nobody prefers a moderate site particularly Google. Studies show that guests anticipate that a site should stack in two seconds or less. In the event that it takes four seconds or more, guests are probably going to bob. While skip rates are not an immediate factor of SEO, they frequently connote a greater issue, for example, poor or unessential content (which, as you most likely are aware, are the central points for SEO).

Another SEO best practice is diminishing the quantity of 404 mistakes decently well. A 404 blunder is the thing that happens when a client arrives at a non-existent page. This can happen on account of a wrecked connection, an erased page, or a mistyped URL. An excessive number of 404 mistakes adversely sway SEO positioning. On the off chance that a client arrives at a 404 connection, he'll likely hit the back catch, come back to the internet searcher, and select another site in lieu of yours. This reveals to Google that your content isn't increasing the value of your catchphrase. On the off chance that it happens enough, you'll see a decrease in positioning.

Ultimately, ensure you have a sitemap. Having a sitemap isn't only an SEO best practice, it's Marketing 101. Not exclusively will it assist guests with exploring your webpage, it will help Google effectively slither your page and file your site.

Clearly, you need to place yourself in the best position to rank well on Google. However, it's essential to remember that keeping up a decent online nearness goes past search rankings.

The above fundamentals of the SEO are significant in helping your site fit in with Google's website admin rules, which will, thus, procure you better web search tool rankings. What's more, consistency with these rules is presently more significant than any time in recent memory, particularly once the Mobile-First Index framework is completely turned out in 2019.

Regardless of what Google says thinks or does, there are numerous SEO-related undertakings you shouldn't ignore. Some are basically savvy to do in light of the fact that they don't influence you contrarily, and some are only perfect for more noteworthy's benefit.

Who should write your content

A life without any content, how would it be? If we imagine the absence of any type of content, what would the websites be representing on their webs? And the marketing campaigns with no content?

Similarly, the display of visual news without any written content might look awful to you. These things are surely hard to digest ....

In addition to this, on the off chance that there would be no content writers on the planet? Would there be anyone with the ability to writing influential content with the great use of a combination of words? Factually, both the content writers and the content are interlinked with one another and are considered essential for each individual on this planet to continue moving with any particular thing such as marketing campaigns, websites, blogs and etc.

It might not be easy for everyone to be a content writer or pursue content writing as a profession. As before you start claiming your success regarding content writing, you need to do a lot of practice. Undoubtedly, it is just like a car with no driver which reduces the possibility of the car being driven in the right direction. I still reckon if you agree with me at this point or not. But, I believe the majority of people do agree.

Now, I would like to discuss what basically a content writer is. Any individual upholding the capability of writing good and well-written content and provide it to you is a good content writer demonstrating uniqueness and engagement in his or her writing skills. Although the term writing tends to be a vast topic to be discussed, today, I am going to share 20 possible and important skills that one needs to have if he claims himself as a successful content writer.

In particular, in order to be a good content writer you must show obedience. Factually, it is primarily about being good all the way all the time. Some specific areas that the content writer must demonstrate an expert is should include:

1. Good Knowledge of Reader:

With no doubt, communication is considered as an activity among two individuals and the one who tends to ignore the necessity of this communicative approach and writes in a deliberate manner might not be a successful writer. If you are unaware of what to write about and have no idea about your readers then you might tend to throw an arrow regardless of any aim. Right before you start writing, you need to do some market research to have an idea about your audience like other people through the use of persona of buyers and different methodological approaches.

Understanding the reader's needs and develop the ability to align the content in the manner audience prefers to read, one of the key factors is readers that leads you to the development of amazing skills in being a good content writer. For instance, this merely does not mean to allow you writing a memorandum to your boss neither a love letter to your boss. This does not make sense at all, right?

Yes, writing some valuable content for your unknown audience will help you in finding your target audience i.e. who intends to receive your piece of paper. Knowing your reader is important for the creation of content with not only the purpose of letting it be accepted but get shared also.

2. Knowing What You Actually Want to Say

Things become easier when you know what to say resulting in clear-cut subject and topic. Which leads to an interesting and high-quality content. Once, you become aware of your audience, it surely becomes easy and assists you in deciding what you want to share and what others want to listen to.

For instance, if your primary audience or readers are men then you cannot write on topics such as natural beauty. Similarly, if your target readers are women then you can simply write about the ways for muscle gain. I hope, this makes sense to you. Such differences assist you in deciding what should be said and for whom.

The only reason why get stuck while writing anything is that you are unaware of the facts and figures you need to mention. On the off chance that you stall out while composing a section, the explanation might be that you don't have the foggiest idea what you need to state.

importance of content

On the off chance that you are getting befuddled and can't express a sentence to your reader, at that point be guaranteed that you in all probability still don't have the foggiest idea what you are expounding on. To defeat this, you should be extraordinary with your diagnostic and relational abilities. You have to know how you can pass on the thoughts in your mind and clarify the importance between them.

3. Following the Readability Principles

Your content ought to address your reader in a way that can be effectively comprehended. This isn't simple however is basic for being an effective essayist. The High-Five Readability Formula is:

Be Direct with Your Readers

Address your readers like you are having a discussion with them. For instance, if your readers utilize the word 'you' yet as an author, you utilize the word 'we' or 'I'. This guarantees you are talking straightforwardly to your readers and that everything happening is in an immediate tone of discourse. It will likewise enable the reader to constantly and reliably read your content.

Utilize an Active Voice

Utilizing a functioning voice makes your point more clear and increasingly explicit with your readers.

Keep It Optimized and Simple

You may have over and overheard that less complex is better. Be straightforward at every possible opportunity, yet don't talk down or babble in your content. Readers appreciate long reviews, however, in the event that they recognize that you are hauling the theme, they will rapidly explore from your content to some other content.

Adhere to a Single Idea

It is outright craftsmanship to stay predictable with the point you are discussing. For instance, at this moment you realize we are discussing the fundamental aptitudes for being an effective content author. You have to set up a thought in a way that makes it looks solitary (for example try not to over-burden or mistake the reader for other, interrelated thoughts).

4. Continually Being Original

Being remarkable is the pith of being unique, particularly when it applies to content. Being one of a kind is an obligatory quality, in view of reader request, yet in addition since it is basic for SEO purposes.

Posting copy content on the web will build your odds of Google identifying it, and the outcome is that you may get punished. That, yet on the off chance that you duplicate somebody the postings of somebody in different fields, such as advertising, you could be sued for trademark and copyright encroachment. These are not kidding and exorbitant wrongdoings, so you should be unique - with your words as well as with your thoughts also.

Here is "Matt Cutts, a product engineer from Google, depicting how to copy content recognized by Google is taken care of and slaughtered"

5. Giving Answers to the Questions

Posing inquiries all through your content and furnishing your readers with the quick and appropriate answers is an incredible method to keep your reader connected with your content.

The core principle of writing content to grow the knowledge of the readers. And you being a reader, mine purpose of writing the content through use of the initial introduction paragraphs.

Due to this reason, you as a reader have continued to read up till here and onwards.

6. Connecting the Dots

Once again, one of the key factors in the determination of the skills that any good writer pursues is the ability to connect the dots i.e. use of interlinked topics and the content that you would have written in the paragraphs. It is considered quite important due to the reason that if I next start talking about toothpaste hacks then you will surely stop reading. But, no need to be worried. I will surely stick to my point.

7. Summarizing Words

The capability of summing up any particular thought or idea such as the ocean in a cup is the key required for content writing. This mainly requires precise use of words from first to last word of your content with a specified and clear conclusion.

Ignoring this point might turn out to be a serious matter to focus on. What you need to do is to learn to summarize the content including an overview of the key ideas through the use of themes and keywords.

8. Sourcing Information and Citations

Readers will just accept what your content says insofar as you furnish them with right and exact data. You should be sufficiently bold to interface your content with its unique sources and to make reference to them any place required.

This could likewise incorporate outer connecting. By connecting out to extraordinary sources, it implies you are telling web indexes that you have something extremely incredible to appear. Here's "Cyrus Shepard, from MOZ, clarifying the significance of connecting to outer sources from the SEO point of view:"

9. Showing restraint toward Research Skills

This is the basic leadership point - in the event that you have persistence and phenomenal research and logical aptitudes, you're your odds of turning into a fruitful content essayist are higher. In content composition, the examination component is significant.

It doesn't make a difference whether we're alluding to catchphrase examine, theme look into, specialty investigate or some other sort of research, you just need to stay tolerant without getting overactive, in light of the fact that doing research on the web isn't a simple undertaking and can once in a while become discouraging and disappointing.

10. Assessing Your Content as a Reader Would

When you have finished your content, you have to step back, slowly inhale and audit your content without inclination. You have to consider a reader recognizing botches in content. By doing this, you end up with mistake-free content from a syntactic outlook, yet additionally from thoughts one also.

11. Swapping Writing Styles

Continually composing on a similar theme and in a similar specialty isn't useful for your wellbeing. It can likewise slaughter your inventive abilities. A conceivably effective essayist must switch the composing types and specialties to various subjects to improve their capacity to break new ground, just as to build their insight. Work on composing on 360-degree inverse themes to pick up these aptitudes!

12. Composing on Relevant and Vibrant Subjects

As an across the board content essayist, you should have the option to in a split second adjust to any pattern, regardless of whether it be from the news or web-based life, and have the option to begin composing on it.

Readers will consistently look through the web about pertinent and interconnected stories to whatever content they were perusing. That is the reason a content author should have the option to utilize this aptitude, to keep readers locked in.

13. Thinking About WordPress and Search Engine Optimization (SEO)

Try not to get discouraged, you just need to know the fundamentals. There is an assortment of WordPress topics accessible with default robotized capacities where you just need to introduce a module to satisfy your needs.

Be that as it may, you should know the urgent SEO nuts and bolts in the event that you plan to be a star content author. The calculations that decide how web crawlers work are continually being refreshed and the best content journalists need to comprehend them so as to effectively exploit them.

The one center that remaining parts reliable steady is the high caliber of the content. On the off chance that you can effectively compose great, quality content, at that point this is something you needn't be worried about.

14. Utilizing Social Media

Long-range interpersonal communication locales work more like a tool than only a center for meeting various individuals from an assortment of spots. Numerous entrepreneurs see every single social medium all in all markets. Many showcasing organizations contribute incredible entireties of cash on advancing items and brands utilizing web-based social networking advertising. Internet-based life is an extraordinary method to make an informal.

Regarding content, online networking is an important tool for leading viral content promoting. The acknowledgment of your name and work is significant and the utilization of internet-based life locales in the proper manners makes it conceivable. You should be great at building individual associations with individuals.

Trying out your plans to individuals along these lines not just forms your audience and handles client consideration, yet fabricates associations with specialty related individuals and bloggers. Furthermore, internet-based life and SEO now work like 2 bits of a jigsaw confound - on the off chance that you perform well via web-based networking media, at that point your content will appear in web indexes also.

15. Language Skills

You have to have great language abilities on the off chance that you need to be a decent content author. These aptitudes should comprise of:

- Spelling

- Language structure

- Word Usage

On the off chance that your language aptitudes are feeble, don't simply sit back. Keep composing basically in light of the fact that it will improve your language aptitudes. You can likewise partake in any of the free language instructional classes that are accessible on the web.

16. Creating Ideas and Grabbing Attention

Creating thoughts is probably the greatest test of the present time. Not every person can concoct new thoughts that trigger the brains of readers and catch their eye. Yet, that being stated, you ought to never fear coming up short with the thoughts you do have.

Keep conceptualizing them and afterward investigate which ones were well-acknowledged by the readers and which ones became famous online by methods for a mutual trigger - for example, content that sticks out and is shared, generally via web-based networking media. You have to realize how to utilize eye-catching procedures, similar to the article and blog titling stunts.

For instance, beneath are two titles written to catch the client's eye. Choose for yourself which one you would decide to click.

- How to Increase Website Traffic?

- 10 Proven Ways to Bring 110,928 Guests to Your Website without a doubt!

17. Being Persistent

Regardless of whether you are a consultant or a staff author, you have to stay constant with your composition. It is totally typical to at times get tired and baffled with everything identified with composing. During those occasions, you may even choose to stop in an undertaking.

In any case, for somebody who needs to be an expert content author, this is something you simply need to endure so as to conquer it. You won't succeed in the event that you ceaselessly quit in your tasks, so you should have the right stuff set up to face new difficulties and manage the unforeseen.

18. Performing Frequent Content Updates Without Hesitation

Web search tools typically don't support locales that don't refresh their content all the time. On the off chance that you possess a site or blog, you should ceaselessly refresh your content with the goal that the crawlers continue getting the sign that you are alive. Try not to stop for a second in doing as such, on the grounds that consistent refreshing causes you to keep up higher internet searcher rankings.

A significant number of the best content sites are refreshed normally in order to keep up their rankings and position. All the more critically, these essayists want to furnish their readers with the most exceptional data. All in all, how regularly would it be a good idea for you to refresh? This is totally at your caution, contingent on the nature and specialty of your site. For the most part, rolling out month to month content improvements is adequate!

19. Making Calls to Action

Invitations to take action (CTAs) are one of the most nonexclusive approaches to catch client eye and increment viewership. A decent content essayist should realize how to make drawing in CTAs which incite clients to react eagerly.

Here is a case of a CTA method received by the popular online business site, Shopify, which expanded their business ten times since they began offering free preliminaries to their clients.

20. Conveying

You have to try sincerely as a content author, regardless of whether you have great relational abilities or not. You should realize the most ideal approaches to speak with your readers. Regardless of whether it's by including pictures, infographics, recordings or insights. you have to do it on the grounds that eventually, you need to convey what you're thinking in the most ideal manner conceivable.

A few readers see better by perusing, some by tuning in and some by review. You have to guarantee you can keep your correspondence buzzing with an assortment of reader types. Simply avoid pointless stock photography!

To condense, you have to guarantee you are OK with the 20 beforehand recorded abilities. On the off chance that you feel that none of your aptitudes are inadequate with regards to, at that point why pause? Get moving and hit the market solid with your astounding content composing abilities. Trust me, there is nobody who can prevent you from being a fruitful content essayist inside your industry insofar as you are sure with the range of abilities portrayed.

Conclusion

Nothing affects the reader most despite the quality of the content, regardless of who else is the writer or what content strategy has been used or implemented. The copywriting is primarily associated with any specified type of content in order to get potential results. You might understand the key important factors that are required by every marketing specialist who significantly upholds the capability to convince you for the purchase of whatever the person is selling.

In the era of digital marketing, the place where every individual such a publisher with the ability to write a quality content might come across as one of the most important impression that is related to what the reader wants to listen to.

Boosting the process of creation of any content while ensuring the use of all competitive advantages of a writing team and heighten the content quality is thought to be mutually exclusive. Good planning is one only thing that is required. , Therefore, it is one of the requirements for you to search that content niche with low supply but increased popularity. This is the decline in the content strategy that is considered as an important part from which the authors generate revenues.

The prevalence of one particular issue initiates due to the presence of online business supported by a number of factors. It might be possible for you being a blogger who has confusion regarding the selection of some key points that are required to complete the competitors.

Despite it is all about the content's nature depending on your ability to characterize things required for an increase in the development of the audience.

The selection of the right point for illustration of your blog tends to be indispensable i.e. the requirement of composing the post in such a way that it draws the attention of the reader. Additionally, such readers will surely help you in the development of your audience.

The composition of a decent entry of the blog is known for the implication to convince the reader that the post is only for him.

Every writer requires a clan which is considered quite common and obvious. Holding up with the same data as of the other journalists and watch them getting success, currently, it is all about the standards but not the characters which make the procedure work. The existence of all writers in the world of content writing is completely based o staying up with the latest trends of the industry and gauges to pursue the appropriate productions.

You might have lose your courage to convince the readers to read the article which tends to be a noticeable artistic expression by itself. But, in any case, if you do not do well, you might be breaking your trsust over readers and your potential to produce quality content with advertisers, endorsers, leads and any other one. While getting your content published, there are editors and proofreaders you polish your content as any writer might not be able to notice some minor mistakes while writing. Considering the example of an office setting, you can surely have a review of what you have written is fine or not or on the other way, you can surely employ an agency like Wordy.

Making efforts not to compose the content which lacks the potential to grab the attention or hack the mind of the reader. Writing a short story might significantly address the spirit of convincing the readers to give a response right at the moment. Your developed connection with one particular story might lead to the inspiration of a second story.

Considering the firms, who deal with the construction of a hostage, the presence of the steadfast audience implies you for the reduced investment of energy and exertion selling.

However, there are many ways to help you getting started. Currently, you might uphold a number of strategies that can be significantly used for the development of your audience and some others who tend to retain their audience for a large amount of content.

The first and foremost that you need to focus on is primarily the opening of your blog, ebook, article or any other content writing product. Start with such a selection of words that readers get obliged to read the whole content. This can only be done through awareness about what they actually want to hear.

Everything is possible, the thing that is solely required is your courage to take a step and the passion to lead the way. As discussed in the content above, your key focuses and your audiences are the ones who significantly derives your way to success. Due to advances in technology, things have been much easier. You are able to find almost everything at one-click. The technology has surely revolutionized our lives and is consistently doing so.

Thus, it is all up to you, how you use this technology to get to your target audience, to promote your content, to get it updated, to edit it when required, and to bring positive changes in the lives of your reader by knowing and completely their demands. This can only be done when you would have done market research and awareness of what people seek out.